MARILYN SEGAL, Ph.D., is Professor of Developmental Psychology and the director of the Family Center, Nova University, Florida. She is the author of seven books and a series of television programs on early childhood.

DON ADCOCK, Ph.D., is a Child Development and Parenting Specialist who has co-written four books with Dr. Segal.

PRENTICE-HALL INTERNATIONAL, INC., *London*
PRENTICE-HALL OF AUSTRALIA PTY. LIMITED, *Sydney*
PRENTICE-HALL OF CANADA, LTD., *Toronto*
PRENTICE-HALL OF INDIA PRIVATE LIMITED, *New Delhi*
PRENTICE-HALL OF JAPAN, INC., *Tokyo*
PRENTICE-HALL OF SOUTHEAST ASIA PTE. LTD., *Singapore*
WHITEHALL BOKS LIMITED, *Wellington, New Zealand*

A SPECTRUM BOOK

PRENTICE-HALL, INC., Englewood Cliffs, N.J. 07632

Marilyn Segal
Don Adcock

JUST PRETENDING

Ways to Help Children Grow Through Imaginative Play

Library of Congress Cataloging in Publication Data

SEGAL, MARILYN M.
    Just pretending.

    (A Spectrum Book)
    Bibliography: p.
    Includes index.
    1. Play.   I. Adcock, Don.   II. Title.
HQ782.S39   155.4'18   81-1089
ISBN 0-13-514067-6   AACR2
ISBN 0-13-514059-5 (pbk.)

A SPECTRUM BOOK

10   9   8   7   6   5   4   3   2   1

All photographs are by William L. Sorchet with the following exceptions: those on pages 24, 38, and 150 are by Marilyn Segal, on pages 44 and 144 by Nick Masi, and on page 41 by Kristin W. Adcock.

Editorial/production supervision and interior design by Frank Moorman
Cover art by April Stewart
Manufacturing buyer: Cathie Lenard

Contents

Preface

"When the Rabbit actually took a watch out of its waist-coat pocket, and looked at it, and then hurried on, Alice started to her feet, for it flashed across her mind that she had never before seen a rabbit with either a waist-coat pocket, or a watch to take out of it, and, burning with curiosity, she ran across the field after it, and was just in time to see it pop down a large rabbit hole under the hedge ..."

The appeal of fantasy is universal. Adults as well as children enjoy slipping through the rabbit hole with Alice and escaping the bonds of reality. For us as adults these flights of fantasy are usually short-lived, but for young children they are a way of life. In *Just Pretending* we take a close look at the imaginative play of children during that brief period in the preschool years when fantasy is out in the open.

The basic premise of *Just Pretending* is that imaginative play, because it is so pervasive, plays a critical role in the development of young children. In the first three chapters we take a close look at a selection of preschool children who do a lot of pretending. Our goal is to explore the developmental benefits of pretending. Why do these children spend so much time and expend so much energy on imaginative play?

In each of the first three chapters we provide a different answer to why children delight in pretending. In the first chapter, we view pretending as a way of making friends and we identify ways in which children use imaginative play to develop social skills. In the second chapter, we view pretending as a way of making sense out of the world. Through such play children not only expand their real world concepts, but they learn to use a system of symbols that allows them to think abstractly. In the third chapter, we view pretending as a way of feeling good about yourself. We describe ways in which children use pretending to reexperience happy events, to gain a sense of power, and to overcome bad feelings.

These different views of pretending complement rather than contradict each other, demonstrating that imaginative play serves a variety of purposes and provides a variety of benefits.

In the second part of the book we seek to answer another question: What kind of environment allows pretending to flourish? We do not believe that imaginative play develops automatically or inevitably. Its growth is affected by the quality of a child's environment, and a critical element in that environment is the role that adults take. Again, we discuss this issue from three interrelated perspectives:

The Adult as Observer
The Adult as Planner
The Adult as a Model

At the end of each chapter we present a brief summary of a relevant research study. These threads from the literature on imaginative play are pulled together in a final chapter, where we consider how our findings both support and challenge the research of others.

The raw material for *Just Pretending* is derived from two years of observation. In order to get an authentic picture of imaginative play we used natural settings as a base for observation. Thirty-six children were selected from a pool of volunteer families and their pretend play observed over a six-month period, both at home and at school. These observations were supplemented by weekly telephone conversations with the parents of the children.

The families in the study were drawn from different and socioeconomic levels, ethnic groups, and geographic regions. However, the sample is not typical because our study procedures required volunteer parents who were both good observers and careful reporters. These parents were especially interested in pretend play, and their children displayed a rich repertoire of play behaviors. In this sense *Just Pretending* is about the potential for imaginative play in the lives of young children.

The most interesting imaginative play occurred at home and therefore most of the data reported in this book comes from a home setting. However, we strongly believe that the information we have collected is applicable to a school setting as well. It is our hope that teachers of young children will be as intrigued as we are by the phenomenon of pretending, and that imaginative play will be given a prominent place in preschool curricula.

Parents and teachers who are concerned about the development of young children are often tempted to teach academic skills. They are concerned about performance in school and feel compelled to spend time with children teaching numbers and letters. Children who are actively engaged in pretending are preparing for school in a different way. They are learning to play cooperatively with other children, to cope with stress, and to experience the world from a new perspective. They are developing a symbol system which helps them to separate the concept of a thing from the thing itself, and serves as the cornerstone for abstract thought. Most important, children who engage in active pretending are developing imagination and creativity—so that one day they may learn what has not been discovered and imagine what has not been created.

ACKNOWL-EDGMENTS

We would like to extend a very special thank you to Dr. Susan Talpins and Dr. Wendy Masi who served as research associates for *Just Pretending*. Susan and Wendy have not only served as observers and recorders of pretend play but have also played a major role in the selection and analysis of anecdotal material. In a very real sense Wendy and Susan have been the midwives of *Just Pretending*, communicating with families, interpreting child behavior, evaluating rough drafts, assisting in a thousand different ways with the delivery of the manuscript.

DEDICATION

To Erik, Kori, and Jennifer—three special children who have shared with us their charm, their creativity, and their fun-filled fantasy world.

JUST
PRETENDING

PART ONE

THE BENEFITS OF IMAGINATIVE PLAY

Chapter One

A Way of
Making Friends

"Good morning, Foggy Winds!" Jamie announced cheerfully. "You ready to go on a bus ride to school? Do up your seat belt. It's a bumpy ride." At this point Jamie's father came in the room and was about to sit on an empty chair. "No! No! Don't sit there, Daddy. You'll squash Foggy Winds!" A little later Jamie's parents talked about the incident, trying to figure out if Jamie really believed that Foggy Winds was real. "Jamie probably knows he's pretending," his mother decided, "but it's very convenient to have a playmate who appears whenever you need him."

In this chapter we examine ways in which children use pretending to make friends and develop social skills. First we explore the different ways in which children use their imagination to create pretend friends. Next we see how imagination helps children build a rapport with real friends. As we recount some typical pretend play episodes between children and their friends, we discover how pretending helps children acquire different perspectives, learn cooperation, and become sensitive to the feelings of other people.

MAKING FRIENDS WITH OBJECTS

"Don't worry. I know you are for cigarettes. Grandma will be back soon and she'll put cigarettes in you."

Angela's remarks were directed toward an ashtray in her home. She showed concern for the ashtray because it had been filled with bits of crumpled paper instead of the usual cigarettes. Jamie attributed similar feelings to a piano:

"You're a nice piano. Don't cry out loud!"

"Okay, piano—I will sing a song to you. You're a nice piano. Don't cry out loud."

Erik felt sorry for a frog wastebasket that he met in a department store. When it was time to leave the store he turned to it and said apologetically, "Bye-bye, basket. I have to go now."

It is not unusual for children, especially younger preschool children, to talk to objects in this way. The children seem to imagine that the objects are feeling sad or lonely and feel a strong identification with them. The objects are seen as companions to be sympathized with when they are handled roughly, ignored, or abandoned.

Although preschool children do console objects, usually it is the other way around. Object companions provide security and solace to children. These security objects come in different forms. They may be objects that are associated with a parent, such as a set of keys, or something just purchased at the store, such as a new toothbrush or a bottle of glue. They may be objects that a child finds especially exciting to handle, like an oil can or a hairy coconut. Whatever the reason, it is clear that they have become security objects when a child takes them to bed, wants to bring them to the table, or clings to them in a new situation.

The most common object companion is a blanket. Babies on their way to sleep stroke the silk border of a blanket or rub the fringe between their fingers. This tactile stimulation gives them a sense of comfort. In time the blanket becomes a symbol of comfort and is elevated to the status of a friend:

"Mommy, Silky's finished his washing. Take him out of the dryer. He's all dried up."

Silky was Ken's name for a faded baby blanket. Whenever his mother suggested that Silky was looking rather dirty, Ken was immediately on guard. He refused to leave the laundry room until Silky was safely out of the dryer. As he carried Silky back into his own room, his mother heard him mumble, "Okay, Silky, now you're clean for a long, long time."

A blanket companion like Silky is a substitute for parents, protecting the child when the parent is missing. As children become more aware of a parent's role, it is natural for the blanket to be given new characteristics as well:

"Will Silky be proud of me if I hang from the monkey bars? Will Silky be angry if I don't go to sleep? Will Silky be happy if I do well in school?"

Just like a parent, Silky approved and disapproved of behavior, but as an extra parent, Silky also served as a buffer when Ken got scolded by his real parents. "I'm going to tell Silky on you," Ken threatened his father when he was made to pick up his toys.

Occasionally we find children who use their own hands or feet as readily available object companions. Angela, a very imaginative three-year-old, talked to her hands quite often. Sometimes the conversation was casual. "See, hands, that's a dog over there. And up there, that's the sky." At other times, her hands got scolded for doing something naughty. "No, no, hands. You are not supposed to do that. Don't do that or you're going to get a spanking."

In a variation of the theme, Myla, at four-years-old, acted out a playful dialogue between her two feet.

Foot # 1: My shoe is off. Is your shoe off?

Foot # 2: My shoe's off. Is your sock off?

Foot #1: Yes, my sock's off.

Foot # 2: Good night, foot.

Foot # 1: Good night, other foot.

Although young children develop attachments and carry on conversations with blankets and other objects, these objects are not likely to take on a personality. They may be friends of a sort, but they do not look or act like friends. They have no eyes to see with, no mouth to talk with, no legs to run with. They neither sleep nor eat. An object companion that seems more lifelike is needed, and to this end dolls were invented ages ago. Dolls and stuffed animals represent a special kind of object that has been designed for the purpose of companionship. They have resulted from the spontaneous human tendency to use objects as imaginary friends. The relationships that young children develop with these dolls and stuffed animals far exceed, both in duration and intensity, their relationships with other objects.

MAKING FRIENDS WITH DOLLS AND STUFFED ANIMALS

Dolls and stuffed animals serve two different functions for young children. On the one hand, they represent substitute babies that require care and comfort. On the other hand, they serve as friends providing companionship, protection, and support. The two functions are usually intermingled to some extent. Dolls that are treated as babies occasionally take on the characteristics of friends, and conversely, dolls that generally are companions may be reduced in status from time to

A doll as a substitute baby.

time. The same doll or stuffed animal may even be used in a dual role, but more often it is primarily either a baby or an equal.

Laura's favorite doll was named Velvet, and she was clearly Laura's baby:

> "Did you have a nice sleep, Velvet? Oh, that's good. How about a little lunch? How about something to drink? Can I have a taste of that? Oh, it's so good. Are you ready to go in the stroller?"

Putting Velvet in the stroller, Laura pushed her through an imaginary department store. They were shopping for "baby things." Frequently Velvet had to be changed. Laura especially enjoyed using a wet washcloth or a real towelette to wash Velvet's bottom, and then she dressed the baby in a cloth diaper with real pins.

Although Velvet is the baby in Laura's pretend family, she can be a companion at times. While on the shopping trip, Velvet sat with Laura and her mother in a pretend restaurant. She ordered an apple from the menu and shared the apple with Laura's mother. Then she got some money to spend in the store. As Laura explained, "Velvet needs money in her pockets." Velvet is enough of a peer to share some of Laura's prized possessions, too. When they got home from shopping, Velvet went to sleep in Laura's old crib. Laura gave her a Donald Duck toy, a pocketbook, a nail file, a ring, and a bracelet—just the sorts of things that Laura might wish to have in her own bed.

Being a parent who takes care of a helpless infant is a role that preschool children understand quite well, but they are more interested in their own life situation. For this reason, dolls that are babies tend to grow up quickly as the children project their own predicaments and wishes on the dolls. A doll may be a baby one day, and a four-year-old child the next. Kori, for example, was given a baby doll when her brother was born. At first she treated the doll, whose name was Alyse, as a baby. Alyse's messy habits were duly noted after Kori fed the baby some ice cream:

> "Alyse wants to wash her hands. She got all sticky. She ate her ice cream with her hands instead of a fork. Wasn't that silly? You're supposed to eat ice cream with a fork."

Kori asked for a basin of water and washed Alyse's sticky hands. A few days later, though, Alyse had become Kori's contemporary:

> "Alyse was four on her birthday. She just drinks bottles at night. Oh, Alyse, what's wrong? Wait just a minute. I'll get your bottle. Don't cry, you shouldn't do that."

Although Alyse grew up quickly, Kori continued to play the role of a parent. Dolls that are friends do not need a parent figure around. This distinction between doll baby and doll friend can be seen clearly in Wendy's play. Wendy pushes her baby dolls to the store in a carriage, but her Barbie dolls ride their own motorcycle. The baby dolls are given bottles of milk, but the Barbie dolls serve drinks to themselves as they sit around the pool. In theory, Wendy's dolls are teenage jet-setters, in the style of the stereotypes projected on television. In practice they are substitutes for Wendy's real preschool playmates. The doll's teenage behavior is limited to a few superficial activities. Most of the time, they carry out the same pretend themes that Wendy and her friends enjoy. They pretend to cook, to go bowling, to take a trip on an airplane, etc.

Brian plays with his superhero dolls in much the same way. Despite their superhero identity, Brian treats them as if they were his contemporaries. He moves the dolls around the room, dons his own superhero cape, and spars with each one in turn:

> "I'll be Batman. I'll be Batman. I'll beat you right up—ha, ha. Boom-bow, boom, boom gotcha—gotcha. This is what Hong Kong Phooey does. Hong—Kong—Phooey!!!"

Friends like Brian's superhero dolls or Wendy's Barbie dolls are good for sharing the excitement and danger of a pretend play episode. Doll friends also offer many of the other benefits of real friendship. They give support in scary situations, provide comfort when things are going badly, and serve as a listening post when a child needs someone to talk with.

WATCHING A FRIENDSHIP DEVELOP

While some children fasten on to a favorite doll or stuffed animal as their cherished companion, other children, who are perhaps a bit more gregarious, surround themselves with a collection of friends. Their collection of friends may serve as traveling companions, as an appreciative audience, or as fellow actors in a pretend play episode. Jennifer spends a fair amount of each day traveling around in a car. Before each car ride she decides which friends to take along with her.

> *Mother:* Okay, Jennifer, jump in the car. I'll be late for work.
>
> *Jennifer:* I need my friends.
>
> *Mother:* I have three friends: Raggie, Angela, and Pam.
>
> *Jennifer:* Pam lost her shoe in the elevator. I need lots more friends.
>
> *Mother:* Okay, Sally and Boy are here. Let's go.

Perfectly satisfied by now, Jennifer jumps in the car.

A child's special doll friend may carry over from infancy. Raggie has been Kori's faithful companion since she was old enough to look at a face. On the other hand, the search for just the right doll friend may take considerable time. Zach's family lost their dog, Happy, and Zach needed a new companionion to fill this void. One day he watched a little girl pretending that she had a dog named Muffin, and he decided to have his own Muffin. For the rest of the day, Zach played and talked with the imaginary dog. Muffin sat on the lunch counter when Zach ate and Zach's mother set an extra plate for Muffin to use. Later, Muffin acted like Happy by wandering outside on his own, but this time Zach succeeded in catching his pet:

> "Bad Muffin. When you go outside, tell Zachary, Fuzzy Muffin, nice Muffin."

Muffin turned out to be a momentary companion. In the following days Zach made no mention of him, but a week later he found a toy squirrel at his grandmother's. This time the intense interaction lasted three days. The squirrel was a constant companion, and Zach began to talk for the squirrel in a high squeaky voice. Then the squirrel was replaced by a stuffed zebra called Zebe. Each morning Zebe poked his muzzle in Zach's cereal and ice skated on the counter. Then they went to school, Zach talking for both of them about all the things they would do together. Zebe helped Zach feel comfortable at school, and in return, Zach made sure that Zebe did not get lost:

Zach: Where are you, Zebe?

Zebe: (In a high squeaky voice) I lost.

Zach: You come play with me.

The two remained inseparable friends from that day on, eating, sleeping, and going to school together. Zach's mother had to remember that she had two young children to feed, to take to school, and to tuck into bed at night. Like a true friend, Zebe could even be counted on to take the blame for a bad experience. Zach woke up crying one night and told his mother, "I had a bad dream. Zebe gave me a bad dream."

CREATING INVISIBLE PLAYMATES

We began this chapter with a reference to Foggy Winds, the little boy who lives in Jamie's head. Invisible companions seem to be most common with three-year-olds, particularly firstborn children who do not have many playmates. Parents are curious about these imaginary playmates. How did their youngsters come up with the idea in the first place?

One way to understand invisible playmates is to think of them as a kind of extension of telephone friends. Just about every young child picks up the telephone and pretends to be talking to someone. These conversations are usually short, to the point, and directed at real people:

"Hello, Nana? I want to come to your house. Good-bye."

Even at this early stage children seem aware that the party on the other end of the line is imaginary. They do not listen for a voice on the telephone, and they do not expect real consequences to follow from the conversation. Older preschool children can be seen calling characters that are completely fictional. One child may call a restaurant to order food, another may call a garage to get the car fixed. We overheard such a conversation when Laura was playing with her doll Velvet. Laura was pretending to talk on the phone with another mother:

"Hello, hello . . . I have a baby in my stroller. She's going to sleep. We're going to lunch soon. Do you have a baby?"

Then Laura let Velvet talk to the imaginary baby:

(Laura speaking for Velvet) "Oh, give me six yeses.
I have a mother. Good-bye."

Imaginary telephone companions are often just a passing fancy. They are nameless characters who silently act out a part and then disappear. Yet they illustrate that most preschool children readily accept the legitimacy of an invisible companion. Some children simply go beyond the momentary companionship of a telephone conversation and create a full-time friend.

In Chad's case a telephone conversation actually led to an invisible friend. Chad wanted to play with an older boy in the neighborhood named Stevie. One day he asked his mother to pretend that she was Chad and he would be Stevie. He picked up the phone and said:

"Hi, Chad. This is Stevie. Can you play? I'll be right over."

Then Chad resumed his normal identity and made a noise like an imaginary doorbell. He opened the door and welcomed the invisible Stevie:

"Come in. Let's pretend like we're driving cars because it's raining outside. Put the wipers on. Come—I'll show you how to drive."

More often than not, imaginary friends do not have real counterparts. They appear out of the blue—and parents are suddenly made aware that an invisible child has taken up residence in their home. Parents naturally wonder what function these invisible friends serve. Why do they appear? Invisible friends serve the same function as other imaginary friends. They are playmates, confidantes, and allies against adults. They provide protection in stressful or scary situations.

INVISIBLE FRIENDS AS COMPANIONS

Foggy Winds, Jamie's imaginary friend, appears to function most of the time as a malleable companion. Jamie's favorite activity is riding the schoolbus and sitting next to the driver. At home he pretends to ride the bus and Foggy Winds rides with him:

"Okay, now, Foggy Winds. Get your things ready. It's time to ride on the bus. Sit right there beside the driver and don't forget your seat belt."

Jamie also likes to pretend that he is flying to Boston to visit his grandfather and Foggy Winds naturally accompanies him. One day Jamie's mother overheard these enigmatic instructions, which seemed to be addressed to Foggy Winds:

"Come on, we're going to the pair. We're going to the pair and see Dr. Fowler. I'll hold your hand."

At Jamie's school the children are paired when they take walks or go from one place to another. Apparently Jamie has extended this system to home. Foggy Winds is his partner for excursions originating at home. Foggy Winds is no ordinary traveling companion though. He can make himself small enough to ride in Jamie's hair if necessary.

Children who have invisible friends often seem to be creating a duplicate of themselves. The invisible friend is a mirror image of the child, as if the child has split himself into two people. Foggy Winds, for example, first appeared in the following conversation between Jamie and his father:

Father: Where's Jamie?

Jamie: I don't know.

Father: Who are you?

Jamie: I am a little boy named Foggy Winds. I will go and find Jamie. He's at the store getting oranges. Here he is. I finded him. Hurray for Jamie!

Jad is a firstborn child like Jamie, and in this case the actual name of the invisible friend suggests it is an alter ego. His friend's name is "Ja-Ja." One day Jad was riding down a deserted country road. Jad was alone in the back seat. "Ja-Ja," his mother heard him say, "there are wolves around this place, and don't worry about it, okay? I'll go get my tiger and he'll scare away the wolves." Obviously Jad was talking to himself and his reassurances to Ja-Ja were meant for his own ears.

Ja-Ja's role as alter ego is even more apparent in the following episode. After being refused permission to see "Bedknobs and Broomsticks," Jad sat down on the floor and pretended to hold Ja-Ja's hands.

"You see, Ja-Ja," Jad explained in a tone that resembled his father's, *Bedknobs and Broomsticks* is on much too late, and you need to go to bed on time so you grow up nice and strong." At the end of the conversation with Ja-Ja, Jad felt much better about things. Having an alter ego to take the brunt of bad news helped Jad keep his own ego intact.

INVISIBLE FRIENDS AS PROTECTORS

Brian has an invisible friend named Danny, who plays more of a protector role. During the day Danny is usually working at an imaginary farm, but when Brian goes to the bathroom, Danny suddenly appears in order to help him. In the evening, when it starts getting dark, Danny's presence is even more noticeable. He takes a bath with Brian, joins him during teethbrushing, and follows him to bed. On his way to sleep Brian tells Danny everything that happened during the course of the day.

Children who need someone to take a protector role may select animals rather than people to serve as invisible companions. After seeing the movie "Pete's Dragon," Joey decided that Elliot (the dragon) was living at his house. Elliot slept on the rug in front of Joey's bed and accompanied Joey when he started preschool. On a trip to Disney World, Elliot used his magic power to turn the ghosts in the Haunted House into Joey's friends.

Angela also created an imaginary animal friend to protect her from dangerous things that lurk around the house. Since she is especially afraid of the shower, her friend, who is an invisible dog, stays in there most of the time. When Angela gets in the shower, she pretends to feed the dog some milk from the cap of an aerosol can. Angela also imagines that there is a "factory" (some sort of machine monster) in her house. Whenever the "factory" appears in Angela's room, the dog is summoned from the shower.

CROWDS OF INVISIBLE FRIENDS

Kori and Laura lived in neighborhoods where there weren't too many children. Both girls compensated for the lack of real friends by creating a crowd of pretend friends. Kori created her collection of imaginary friends when she first found out that her mother was pregnant. "I have ten babies in my tummy," she explained to her mother in a confidential tone. Several days later, Kori was sitting in her room thrusting a spoon into thin air. "I'm busy feeding my babies," she explained. "I took them out of my tummy 'cause they are very hungry. Come here Akie, Mimi, and all the little sisters."

Laura's collection of imaginary friends had even more unusual names. Gerch and Humble made their first appearance one morning when Laura and her mother were cleaning up the house. Laura announced in a very serious voice that someone was knocking at the door.

Mother: I didn't hear it. Let's go and see if someone is there.

Laura: I go to the door with you.

Mother: Oh—we must be mistaken. Nobody is here.

Laura: Humble and Gerch are here. Come in Humble and Gerch. You want some crackers and cheese? You want some water without any chlorine in it?

After this first appearance, Humble and Gerch were frequent visitors. Sometimes they came alone; at other times they brought along their pals, Meemar and Beeboo. For the most part Laura used her imaginary companions as company at her tea parties or as companions on her pretend excursions. Here is a typical monologue:

"Okay, Humble, sit down on the riding couch. Here's your pocketbook. I'll give you some of my money. I'll put it in your pocketbook. You can keep the money. Here is your picture. Put it in your pocketbook. See my trick, Humble. I'm walking on the pillows."

The oddity of many of the names given to invisible friends alerts us to the fact that these friends are very much the personal creations of young children. Parents and other adults are granted only limited access to this private world. As Jad explained to his mother, "You can't talk to Ja-Ja. He can't hear you." Even well-meaning parents find themselves inadvertently sitting or stepping on an invisible friend. They forget to open the door for the friend, or they close the door in its invisible face. The presence of an invisible friend is under the exclusive control of the child, who is the friend's sole translator and link with the rest of the world.

The child who develops an intimate relationship with an invisible friend may act unusual, perhaps even bizarre, at times. In reality, though, the child is only traveling a bit further down a path that nearly all preschool children explore. Between the ages of two and five children become very aware of friendship, and they seek to make friends. It is inevitable that their newly discovered powers of imagination will be employed in this effort. Some children will find object companions while others will make friends with dolls, stuffed animals, or characters in a story. Those who continue to pursue the possibilities of imaginary friendships will find invisible friends.

In all of these situations young children are fulfilling a primitive but basic notion of friendship. A friend is someone who is always there when you feel alone, always does what you want to do, and always understands you perfectly because he is exactly like you. Of course, real friends can never be this compliant or compatible, and real friendships go beyond self-interest. But for young children who are just learning to extend themselves in friendship, an imaginary relationship is an ideal starting point. As children learn to share experiences with other people imaginary friendships will be replaced by real ones.

One of the easiest and most enjoyable ways for young children to share experiences with other people is to pretend with them. Let us look at how imaginative play promotes real friendships.

PEOPLE AS FRIENDS

For young children friendship means physical contact. They hug and caress dolls, stuffed animals, and other imaginary friends. Real friends get the same treatment. They are hugged, snuggled against, and jumped on. As we will see, imaginative play offers a good way to express and enjoy physical closeness with other people. This physical contact adds a new level of excitement and intensity to the play.

Real people also add a higher level of intellectual excitement to pretending. Play themes are more interesting and more sophisticated when other people join in. When it comes to pretending, two (or more) heads are certainly better than one.

Finally, pretending with other people helps a young child learn how to make and maintain a friendship. Not much social skill is needed to make an imaginary friend. On the other hand, real friends must be respected for their own point of view. They need to be listened to, consulted, and even forgiven from time to time. Imaginative play provides a framework in which it is relatively easy to build mutual respect by resolving differences of opinion and coming up with a cooperative plan. Real friends who play a role in a young child's imaginative play fall into two broad categories—adult friends and peer friends. The kind of imaginative play that occurs with these two types of friends is quite different. Therefore, each type of friend makes a unique contribution to a young child's social world.

MAKING FRIENDS WITH ADULTS

Adult friends play different roles in a pretending situation. They may be participants, entertainers, or an appreciative audience. Let us look first at adult friends as participants. For most children the adult friends who participate most often with them are their parents.

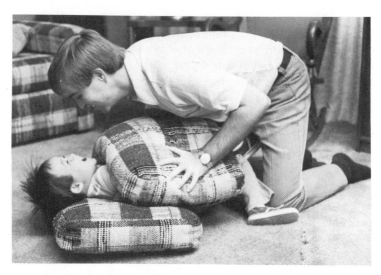

Terry and his father playing sandwich.

In nearly every family there are ritualized pretending games that allow children to enjoy close physical contact with their parents. At Zach's house, the game "I'm gonna get you," which parents play with toddlers, had become a form of imaginative play. His mother's embrace was considered an imaginary jail, and in order to break out of the jail Zach had to utter the magic command, "Open Sesame." In a similar way, lifting children up high becomes an imaginative experience, like riding on an elevator or reaching an imaginary mailbox. Wrestling also is recast into an imaginary mold. Both Terry's and Brett's families, for example, saw wrestling as a way to make an imaginary sandwich. At Terry's house two couch cushions were the bread, and the person in between the cushions was the filling. At Brett's house the whole family cooperated to make the sandwich. Usually Brett's father was the bread. He lay on the floor and announced he was a slice of rye bread or a hoagie roll. Then Brett and his mother lay on top, pretending they were various ingredients like turkey, peanut butter, lettuce, cheese, etc. Amid tickling and wrestling, there were jokes about the strange combinations that resulted: "No, no, not peanut butter on a turkey sandwich."

Earlier we described Chad's desire to play with an invisible Stevie. It was fun to pretend that he and Stevie were driving in the rain. Yet when we compare that episode with another brief episode involving Chad and his mother, we can see the special satisfaction that comes from physical contact with a real friend. Chad had turned on the record player and asked his mother to join him:

"Come dance with me. That's not how we dance, Mommy. Come down here so I can reach your cheek and we can put our cheeks together."

Often adults play the role of a supportive friend, helping a child find props for a pretend theme and occasionally asking an interested question. This kind of participation certainly enriches imaginative play, and we will discuss it more fully in later chapters. Here we want to focus on the quality of friendship that is shared when parents and other adults wholeheartedly join in the pretending. Let us begin by looking at an extended example that was recorded by Erik's father:

> This morning Erik wanted to build a tent. We made a large tent in his room by placing a four-foot ladder across the tops of two tall chairs and then covering this furniture with his bedspread. Erik got some clothes for cold weather, a snowsuit, snow hat, his new jacket, some clothes hangers, Easter eggs, and half-a-dozen stuffed "friends". Tiki, the cat, got in there with us—he is especially delighted when one of the cats will participate. I contributed two sleeping bags, the stove, camera, flashlight, rope, and bicycle hooks.
>
> Erik put the bicycle hooks together, stretching them between the chairs so that a boundary was formed down the middle of the tent. Erik called the hook arrangement a "trap" for wild animals. We hung the clothes from the ladder and divided up the stuffed animals. Erik changed into his snowsuit and hat so he could sleep with his head outside the tent even though it was snowing. The two musical windup animals were our radios. We wound them up and listened to some radio music.
>
> I suggested drawing stars on the chalkboard easel that was holding up one end of the tent. I drew two stars and Erik turned them into a star bicycle. Then he made a star spaceship, and I made a star rocket ship. I started a nighttime rainbow, which he finished.
>
> Before going to sleep we told a ghost story. The story was about animal ghosts and was modeled on Snow White. Then we commenced sleeping, which consisted of many loud snoring noises. I woke up from a bad dream, thought I had seen a bear in the tent. We decided it was just a bad dream—then Erik had a bad dream—we both complained about each other's sleeping noises. Then Erik thought he heard the Easter Bunny coming. I was directed to be the voice. I made hoppity noises on my pillow and

sang a little song about hopping down the bunny trail in the forest, finding a tent and deciding to leave some Easter eggs for the campers. Erik cautioned me to keep my eyes closed so that the Easter Bunny would not be scared away. Morning came and we found the Easter eggs and admired them.

DEVELOPING SKILLS FOR CONVER- SATION

The most striking characteristic of pretending that involves both adults and children is the prominence of conversation. Because the play revolves so much around conversation, it provides a marvelous opportunity for young children to practice this social skill. Conversation becomes the means for working out a cooperative plan. Cooperation generally is easy when children play with adults because adults tend to go along with whatever suggestions children make.

As the participants talk back and forth, each person's comments lead the other person to think of new thoughts. The play becomes more interesting for each participant as one idea builds on top of another. Erik's father suggested drawing the stars, which in turn caused Erik to think of drawing constellation-type designs. Later Erik's father talked about dreaming that there was a bear in the tent. Erik was inspired to have his own bad dream, but then he changed the idea. The noise of a bear, or a snoring camper, became the welcome noise of the Easter Bunny hopping down the trail.

Typical of this kind of shared play, it is the adult who is subtly taking the lead much of the time. In the imaginary camping trip, Erik's father takes a major role in constructing the tent, gathering the props, and introducing new ideas. Yet underlying the play is a feeling of equality, a mutual willingness to explore the imaginary thoughts of the other person. When Erik places the "trap" for wild animals in the center of the tent, his father does not question his logic. By the same token, Erik accepts his father's idea that the easel represents the sky and that there could be such a thing as a nighttime rainbow.

Despite their compliance, adults frequently tease children when playing with them. This teasing is a kind of pretend aggression that is veiled in good humor. As children learn that the aggression is not for real, they can respond to the humor and enjoy the teasing of an adult.

Jennifer's great-grandfather, who is known by two generations of children as a big tease, had selected Jennifer as a perfect child for teasing. A favorite tease routine began one night when Papa and Jennifer were eating dessert. Papa took a pretend swipe at Jennifer's ice cream and insisted that he ate it all up. When Jennifer began to whine her mother gave her some quick advice, "Instead of whining tell Papa not to tease you." "Don't tease me, Papa," Jennifer scolded as Papa pretended to drink her milk. "Well, then I think I'll take your cookie and feed it to the goldfish," Papa continued. "Don't tease me, Papa," Jennifer countered, holding her cookie and laughing. "Don't tease me" became the major words that helped Jennifer remember that Papa was only pretending; and before long, Jennifer discovered that she could reciprocate and pretend to smoke Papa's cigar.

HAVING FUN WITH ADULTS

Most adults who participate in pretending enjoy the role of entertainer. Many parents entertain their children by telling stories. Kori's father, for example, specialized in bald-headed chicken stories, in which a bald-headed chicken accompanied Kori on all kinds of outrageous adventures. Some parents enjoy making up nonsense rhymes or new songs. Others entertain their children by drawing pictures. The children prove to be a very receptive audience. They laugh at the parent's jokes, listen to their stories, and rarely complain if a rhyme is forced, a drawing is hard to recognize, or a song a bit off-key. Imaginative play is of such interest to young children that an adult entertainer is always welcome. The children consider it a sure sign of friendship when an adult takes the time and energy to enter their imaginative world and entertain them.

Some adults are particularly outstanding in their ability to entertain by pretending. The following description of a typical performance by Zach's grandfather illustrates the depth of real friendship that can be communicated through entertainment:

Zach and his grandfather spend much of their time in the doghouse—together. Their doghouse consists of two card tables. Zach was too shy to show us what was inside the doghouse, so Grandpa gave us a tour. He pointed to a stove where Zach cooks hamburgers and said in a confidential but loud voice, "If he offers you one of those pretend hamburgers, don't eat it. They're terrible! He puts too much pepper on them." The singsong quality in Grandpa's voice signaled that he was not really serious, but he did not smile or give any other indication of joking.

Next Zach wanted his grandfather to catch a toy car when it rolled down an inclined board. Grandpa laid his arm across the bottom of the board to stop the car, but as soon as the car touched his arm, he yelled, "Ouch, ooh, ooh. You broke my arm. Better get your medical kit and fix me up." Zach did not follow up on this suggestion in our presence, but Grandpa described how Zach had been operating on him the other day: "I was really sick. He was pulling out cockroaches, sharks, and a rather large octopus."

Again, not the slightest hint of sarcasm. Grandpa never broke the imaginary mental set.

Grandpa next tried to get Zach to show us the rocket ship that they used to go to the moon. Zach was unwilling, but Grandpa continued talking to us. "If you want a rough ride, try that rocket ship. Awfully rough landings, and the takeoffs aren't very comfortable either." Eventually Zach was enticed into the rocket ship, which turned out to be a closet in one of the bedrooms. As they went into the rocket ship Grandpa commented again, "I don't think he quite knows how to operate this spaceship." Zach countered, "Sometimes it do easy landings." But true to form when Zach pressed a spot on the wall, Grandpa went sprawling on the floor as if he had received a terrific jolt. "Where you gonna land?" asked Grandpa. "On the moon," was the reply. "Make it an easy landing," he pleaded.

Grandpa's style of entertaining was to pretend that Zach was hurting or abusing him. He constantly teased Zach, but the implication of his teasing was that Zach had enormous power over him. In the private imaginary world that Zach and his grandfather shared, Zach was both inept and omnipotent. He was in charge, and he cooked hamburgers or drove a rocket ship with all the incompetence of a four-year-old. Yet Grandpa dearly loved every minute of his suffering. The only consequences of Zach's imaginary bumbling were feelings of exhilaration for both Zach and his grandfather. As we prepared to leave, Grandpa called out a final warning: "Don't ever play poker with Zach—you'll lose the shirt off your back."

Obviously adults do not always have the time, or the inclination, to participate as actively as Zach's grandfather. But even when they choose to remain on the sidelines, adults can encourage imaginative play by being an appreciative audience. From the point of view of a child, a parent who applauds a performance or listens to a monologue is a welcome companion, and this gesture of friendship adds to the joy of pretending.

MAKING FRIENDS WITH OTHER CHILDREN

Imaginative play with peers and siblings differs in mood, tempo, and purpose from imaginative play with adults. These differences are most apparent in monster play. Pretending to be a monster, or to be chased by a monster, is a minor theme when children play with adults. When playing with other children, this theme is paramount. We recorded a typical incident as Joanne and Lauren played on a swing set:

Joanne: Here it is! The monster! I see him coming.

Lauren: We better get out quick. Don't let him see your red skirt.

Joanne: He's a big monster. Run away fast. He's great big huge!

Monster play illustrates the kind of physical communication that occurs when children play together. Wild and vigorous actions spread quickly through the group, as each child tries to top the others. Group solidarity develops that is based more on imitation than on genuine interaction. Shouting, chasing, leaping and darting together—this is the essence of monster play. We watched Brian and a group of school friends transform themselves into monsters during recess. "I'm going to eat you, grr, grr," they shouted as they put their hands up in monster fashion, puffed out their cheeks, and raced around the playground. A boy named Aries was spotted, and Brian led the pack against him, "Come on, let's get him." Aries ran out the gate, but no one followed. The monsters continued to swoop around the playground. The attraction of the fantasy lay in the group movement—the monsters were not really hungry after all.

In the world of imagination monsters are controlled by superheroes. Superhero play therefore is virtually identical to monster play, except that the characters are presumably benign. In reality, superheroes are just as wild and destructive as monsters. We observed a group of children who had been given superhero masks to use in their play. No sooner had they become characters like Wonder Woman, Batman, and Spiderman, than they began to yell and growl. A playhouse made of large interlocking panels was dismantled with contagious enthusiasm. Next the group attacked a cardboard Halloween witch and got so carried away with their superhuman strength that they tore off her head. We tried to calm down an especially wild Spiderman by offering him some blocks of food. But the blocks were strewn around the room as Spiderman voraciously chewed and spit out the pretend food.

As children share these dangerous moments and cooperate in rescue attempts, they are gaining ideas from each other. Yet, when we compare different play episodes, it is obvious that the flow of ideas is much greater when children play with adults. In peer play there is less of a cumulative effect than there is in adult play. Instead of one idea building on another, each idea gets bogged down in a round of imitation.

IMITATION IN PEER PLAY

A group of children was playing with a toy village that had been erected on a vinyl map. The primary idea of the group was to drive toy cars along the roads marked on the map. Naturally, the driving became progressively more reckless. Cars crashed into each other and toppled over the buildings in the village. One child introduced the idea of making a jail for bad cars. Quickly a number of jails were built all over the village and cars put in them. Soon, however, the cars burst out of the jails, knocking them flat, and new jails were demolished by rampaging drivers as soon as they were constructed. The excitement of driving wildly was such a strong magnet that the plot was developed no further.

On another occasion a group of children was playing at a sand table with some blocks and farm animals. With a teacher's help the blocks were used to build a barn. One child wanted to put some animals in the barn in order to keep them warm. Immediately the whole group helped place every animal in the barn, as well as the extra blocks and a number of vehicles. The barn was full to the top. Again, with the teacher's help, a flat roof was added, and one of the children suggested that it snow on the barn. Sand was dropped on the barn. It began as a gentle trickle, but soon it became a virtual avalanche that collapsed the roof, buried the animals, and ended the play.

PLAYING OUT A PLOT

Imaginative play between children is not always characterized by boisterous imitation. A small group of children (rarely more than three or four) who know each other well, may play out a lengthy plot. The companionship that is enjoyed in these cases is similar to the feeling shared by children and adults when they pretend together. Wendy and Jan were close friends who played together daily. One day they spent an hour enacting a birthday celebration. Wendy set the roles:

> *Wendy:* You be Uncle George and I'll be Aunt Alice. Now we got to go shopping.
>
> *Jan:* Uncle George needs a wallet. I got to have a wallet.
>
> *Wendy:* Okay, here's a wallet for you. I got my purse. Let's pretend it's your birthday.

After a rather elaborate shopping excursion, which involved filling a paper bag with various and sundry items, the girls returned to the "house" to celebrate Uncle George's birthday. They wrapped up some of their purchases, and Uncle George opened his presents.

Another of the girls' favorite themes is bowling alley. Wendy and Jan, as Mother and Dad, decide to go bowling with their large-size family of dolls. Once at the bowling alley they have to deal with all kinds of problems. They have to buy tickets for the children, the pinsetting machine breaks, and the bowling ball gets stuck on someone's finger.

Usually the highlight of this bowling fantasy is a lengthy trip to the snack bar.

Even when children approximate the model of adult friendship we see elements that are peculiarly childlike. For example, let us listen to Brandon, a six-year-old, play *Star Wars* with his four-year-old brother. Few adults could enter into this scene of carnage with Brandon's spirit and gusto:

> *Brandon:* Wow, man—what's wrong with Vader?
>
> *Scott:* He got shot—his arm's shot off.
>
> *Brandon:* Well, we've got to make a new arm for him. Vrroomm, vrroomm vroom (making manufacturing noises). Okay, you be careful now, Vader. We're all out of arms.
>
> *Scott:* Help—quick! Luke Skywalker's head is shot off.
>
> *Brandon:* Where's the superglue? Here it is—glue his head on.
>
> *Scott:* Zip—zip. I'm sewing it on.

The play of Ken and Jill, two other siblings, illustrates the same idea. Usually they play out family roles with Jill taking the part of the mother and Ken being the father. Yet the childlike character of their friendship becomes quite apparent when they pretend to be objects. One day they may be trucks and somersault around the house. Another day one of them may pretend to be a tree and the other one the wind, or one will be an umbrella and the other one will duck underneath to get out of the rain. In a really comical routine Jill bends over and turns into a toilet, while Ken sits on her back and flushes the toilet by pulling Jill's pigtails.

LEARNING TO PLAN TOGETHER

Cooperative planning is more of a challenge when children play with each other. First, they must agree on the assignment of roles. Perhaps one reason Wendy and Jan cooperated so well was that Jan was willing to take the male roles. She was willing to be Uncle George when Wendy was Aunt Alice and to be Dad when Wendy was Mother. The solution is not always so straightforward. When John and Brian started to play a superhero-monster game, both wanted to be the superhero Batman instead of the monster Godzilla. They cooperated by both being Batman and then both being Godzilla, each time fighting together against an invisible opponent.

Quarrels over role assignment may stop a pretend episode altogether, but when the children really want to play with each other, some

Kori as server and Jennifer as cook.

compromise is reached. Kori and Jennifer both wanted to cook a dinner of pretend spaghetti, but Kori eventually agreed to be the server rather than the "cooker." Brandon preferred to take the role of paramedic, but he was willing to be the heart attack victim because his younger brother always giggled when given the patient's role. The more experience children have with each other, the more adept they become at assigning roles in an equitable manner.

Once roles are assigned there is still plenty of room for disagreement over how the plot will develop. Wendy and Jan were able to cooperate in developing a story line for their bowling fantasy because they had played out this theme a number of times. They practiced the process of sharing and compromising with each other on a daily basis. When children are not as familiar with each other, or a new theme is being explored, cooperative planning becomes a matter of continual negotiation, as each child tries to pursue his own version of events. In the following example an ordinary kind of house play is occurring on the playground. However, the actors are not used to each other and conflict develops:

Three children are playing in a playhouse. A boy about five is on the ground floor and a younger girl and boy are upstairs. The two floors are connected by a ladder that runs through an opening in the second floor. The boy downstairs is peppering the other children with questions. "Want some chicken, want a drink?" He hands up a pretend drink. "Give me your plates," the boy says.

24

"We're saving them," the girl upstairs replies. She does the talking for them.

Apparently it is the end of the day because they all say good night to each other. After a short night, about one minute, the boy calls upstairs, "Want some breakfast?" He has a supply of blocks that he uses for pretend food and plates. "Hand your plate down." But the girl upstairs has no intention of relinquishing her plates. "Here's a pancake," says the boy, handing up a block. "Want some syrup?" More blocks are handed up. He tries to get them to sleep again, "Good night, have a good night." The girl ignores him and asks for orange juice. "All right, two orange juice coming up."

After the orange juice the boy tries again, "Have a good night's sleep." The girl retorts, "It's not even night yet." "Oh, yeah, I forgot," the boy mutters. The girl yells down, "Hey Mac, what happened to our tooth powder?" He finds a block for toothpaste and also hands up a box, "Here's an air conditioner and a fan." Now he figures it really is time for sleep and says, "You can undress yourselves now—for pretend. I won't look. I'll close my door." The girl ignores him, "Hey Mac, we need some dinner."

Despite the somewhat disjointed nature of the conversation at times, the children in this scene manage to keep the imaginative play going for a long time. Their conflicts are handled on a verbal level. As this example illustrates, the negotiation process that occurs during the imaginative play of preschool children is not very refined. The children try to get their own way by ignoring and flatly contradicting each other. On the other hand, the children do not insist on a consensus either. The play can go on in the midst of disagreement in a manner that might strike an adult as chaotic. The conflict over whether or not it was time to sleep never got resolved, but the pretending continued despite this obstacle. The children's lack of skill in settling a dispute was balanced by their willingness to accept an unresolved conflict.

WORKING OUT DOMINANCE PROBLEMS

Conflicts that occur in peer play go beyond specific issues. Often there is a struggle over dominance. Each child tries to find a spot within the dominance hierarchy while retaining a sense of independence. Imaginative play provides an opportunity to work out dominance conflicts:

"Do up your seat belts," Lisa commanded in a loud, strident voice. "We are not playing policeman—I am your mother. Now do up your seat belts like I said."

Katie, who was pretending to be the baby in the family, grabbed

Lisa's sunglasses. "You give them back, baby," Lisa demanded in a stern voice. "Some babies don't give them back," Katie replied, but she did return them.

Next Katie started to chew on her necklace. "Take that out of your mouth," Lisa warned. We suggested that the baby might be hungry and Lisa relented a bit. "You can chew on your necklace until we get to the restaurant."

Once at the restaurant Lisa and the other children ordered corned beef, but Katie wanted chicken. When everybody else decided to have beans, Katie decided on more chicken. Then for dessert, when the rest of the family asked for chocolate butter ice cream, Katie declared that she wanted just plain chocolate.

Clearly Lisa is a bossy child who insists on dominating the play. Katie, however, has learned to accept a subordinate role without fully sacrificing her own independence. Within her role as baby she is able to resist Lisa's bossiness by grabbing Lisa's sunglasses, chewing on her own necklace, and behaving mischievously. At the restaurant Katie further asserts her autonomy by ordering something different. All in all, she has found a clever way to interact successfully with a big, strong, difficult peer.

Conflicts over dominance are perhaps easier to resolve within a pretend context. The consequences of being defeated are not as crushing as in other situations, at least for children who understand the imaginary character of their play. Luis was a four-year-old who initiated many pretend episodes with his friend Scott. Luis was the dominant member of the pair. In the following scene an imaginary fight between the two friends breaks out, and Luis asserts his dominance:

> *Luis:* I'm going to fight you.
>
> *Scott:* I'm going to put you down.
>
> *Luis:* (Shooting toy gun at Scott) You're dead.
>
> *Scott:* I know. (Falls down but gets up immediately)
>
> *Luis:* I shot you Scott. You're under arrest.

At this point Luis grabs Scott and starts to wrestle with him. They both fall down. David, another dominant child who occasionally plays with Luis, has been shooting repeatedly at both Luis and Scott in a futile attempt to be included in the fight. Now he sees an opportunity to join the fracas, and he jumps on top of Luis. Luis immediately appeals to Scott for help. Despite Scott's help David succeeds in taking away

Luis's gun. Luis staggers to his feet and announces the end of the war, "He wins—he took my gun away."

This episode is typical of dominance conflicts between Luis and David. David is physically stronger and usually gains the upper hand, but Luis maintains his dignity by focusing on the pretend contest. In this instance David is not viewed as a bully, but simply as the winner of the pretend fight.

Carrying on a conversation, planning cooperatively, finding a niche within the dominance hierarchy of a peer group, and coping with aggression—these are some of the social skills facilitated by imaginative play. The interaction is smoother when children play with adults. Adults have a greater repertoire of social skills and they are not competing with children as they play. The lessons come faster and more abruptly when children play with each other. Conflicts are sharp and the rules for settling disputes are primitive. Yet in both situations children develop a foundation for the most important social skill of all—the ability to take a new perspective. As different roles are assumed and different pretend scenes created, the children begin to recognize that other people see the world differently. In the long run imaginative play sensitizes children to the feelings of other people, helping them to become more caring human beings.

FROM THE LITERATURE   In order to measure the effects of training preschool children in sociodramatic play Catherine Rosen (1974) conducted a study with lower middle class kindergarten children.° One of her major hypotheses was that imaginative play promotes cooperation. The author selected four classes, two for the experimental treatment and two for control purposes. She visited each experimental classroom for forty days and played with the children for one hour per day during their free period. Initially she worked with individual children, trying to get them to use toys for role play. When most of the children had grasped this idea, Rosen switched to working with groups, encouraging the children to play out scenes that required cooperative role-taking. She regularly provided props for new pretend situations (such as doctor, mountain climber, firefighter, etc.) and then responded to the themes that emerged spontaneously from the children. The children in the control classes were seen weekly by Rosen for ten weeks during which she showed interest in their play activities but did not try to stimulate role play.

°C. E. Rosen, "The Effects of Sociodramatic Play on Problem Solving Behavior among Culturally Disadvantaged Preschool Children," *Child Development* 45 (1974) 920–27.

Before and after the treatment period the children were tested with the Torrance Group Construction Task and the Madsen Cooperative Board. In the first task a group of three to five children are given 130 interlocking blocks. They are asked to work together for fifteen minutes to construct a specific object, such as a school. In the second task a group of four children is given a board with a pen that is controlled by four strings. Each child operates one string and by cooperating they can make the pen move in any direction.

On the group building task the children in all four classes used more blocks on the posttest than on the pretest but the increase shown by the experimental classes was much more dramatic. The groups in these two classes averaged 85.5 and 123.5 blocks in their structure, versus 24.0 and 26.75 blocks in the two control classes. The children were also rated according to several scales by impartial observers and those who had received training in imaginative play were found to be more cooperative. Using the board with the pen, the children from the experimental classes increased their cooperative behavior more than the control children, even when they were encouraged by the tester to compete. (This was done by telling each child in a group that he would be rewarded if the pen crossed "his" circle.)

Although this study shows a positive relationship between training in imaginative play and cooperative behavior, the results are marred by methodological irregularities. Children could not be assigned randomly to treatment and control groups. In fact, one of the control classes turned out to be systematically different from the other three classes. Because of this difference the scores from each posttest were not compared directly, but instead the change from pretest to posttest was compared. On several measures the control classes showed more cooperative behavior in the beginning. Because they had less room for improvement, the results favoring the experimental classes are weakened.

Chapter Two

A Way of Learning about the World

Pretending is a form of thinking and learning as well as a form of play. Although pretending may seem effortless, it is an intellectually demanding activity. It is not easy to create a pretend reality—both concentration and inspiration are needed to keep the illusion alive. We begin this chapter by discussing how the thinking of imaginative play fits into the larger picture of cognitive development. Pretending represents a critical step in passing from the sensory-motor intelligence of infancy to the symbolic thinking of adulthood. As children pretend they transpose their knowledge into symbolic form, and in the process they begin to understand the distinction between fantasy and reality.

In the second section of this chapter we look at the way preschool children develop a vocabulary for pretending. Just as a speaker needs a vocabulary of words, a pretender needs a vocabulary of pretend symbols. The vocabulary of pretending is not as clearly marked as the words of a language, but it rests on the same ability to think abstractly. Children who are learning to talk are involved in breaking reality apart and representing separate pieces of it with individual words. In the same way children who are learning to pretend are abstracting out actions and objects that can be recreated in imaginative play.

In the third section of this chapter we look at how children use their pretend vocabulary to develop pretend episodes. Again we can use language as an analogy. A single word has meaning, but we are able to express ourselves much more completely when we combine words into sentences and paragraphs. The real purpose in building a vocabulary of words is to communicate longer and more complicated thoughts by combining the words. By combining the words in different ways we create new combinations and express new ideas. Of course, the first sentences of children usually express rather obvious thoughts. The two-year-old who says, "Juice all gone," is using a combination of words to make a stereotypical remark. Within a short time, though, the sentences of children can impress us with their creativity, as in the case of a preschool child who looks at the moon passing behind a cloud and says, "It looks like the moon is melting."

Learning to pretend is similar to learning to speak. Symbols from a basic vocabulary are combined into longer and more elaborate pretend episodes. At first these pretend themes, like first sentences, are simple and not very creative. But again, within a short time, stereotypical themes take creative forms, especially in children who have been encouraged to elaborate their pretend thoughts.

THE INTELLECTUAL VALUE OF PRETENDING

Imaginative play as a way of thinking does not arise in a vacuum. It is built upon the intellectual activity of infants and toddlers. During these early years children experience the world as a medley of sensory impressions. In order to make sense out of these impressions they experiment with different actions and then observe the results. In the process they imitate the actions of other people and explore new ways of making things happen. Imitation and exploration are the twin sources of early knowledge and by the time children are toddlers they are masters of both. In the company of older people, they want to be a part of whatever activity is going on; left alone they want to get into everything within reach.

Imitation and exploration continue to be the major means for learning about the world during the preschool years, and they contribute greatly to the growth of pretending. Preschool children become especially adept at imitating language. Mandy, a young preschool child, listened to her parents doing the crossword puzzle. Later she picked up the crossword puzzle, held a pencil pensively in her hand, and played back bits of the conversation.

"Know another word for boxing? Too many letters. You got to have an 'o' in it."

Preschool children also demonstrate a greatly increased ability to imitate the pretending of other people. A single demonstration of a new pretend idea is often sufficient to stimulate imitative play. Other children are effective models for new ideas too. Jennifer concentrated on using a stethoscope when she played doctor at home, but after watching the other children in her preschool she quickly adopted another instrument as her favorite. "This thing is for examining noses because that's the way Carmen does it," she explained to her mother.

The role of exploration in imaginative play, although not as obvious, is just as important. The exploration of toddlers is pretty crude, with a strong emphasis on emptying, tearing, poking, throwing, etc. Preschool children become increasingly concerned with mastering certain skills through exploration and incorporate these skills into their pretending. Emptying and tearing are replaced by filling and constructing. The nature of the physical world is explored by actually creating a pretend object or a pretend landscape. Chris accompanied her construction of a zoo with a running commentary.

"We'll make a zoo. We need the blocks. Just these animals live in the cage, else they'll fight. The monkey swings from here and jumps here. This is for air (pointing to a hole in the wall of the cage). Now they can go and get some water."

In a similar way the poking and banging exploration of the toddler is replaced by more precise ways of handling tools. Tools like pens and crayons are no longer just for random scribbling and gouging, but also for drawing pretend objects and writing pretend words. Kitchen implements are used to pour pretend drinks, to stir imaginary batter, to roll out cookies, etc. Even workshop tools, which are still difficult for many preschool children to control, are incorporated into imaginative play.

Often exploration helps extend a pretend scene because the children are so interested in manipulating the materials. We saw a good example of this phenomenon when watching two boys play house. David was the father and Chris was the mother, but David stayed home from work in order to help Chris peel the potatoes. The potatoes were lumps of clay that the boys were trying to cut into pieces with plastic knives. Peeling the potatoes engaged their interest for over thirty minutes, and during that time other imaginary events occurred. There was a spider on the ceiling that Daddy David killed and threw in the corner. There was a dragon outside that they slew with a gun. The children were called inside and the door locked to keep out any other monsters. Some mud was added to the potatoes. Although dinner never did get served, the exploration involved in cutting the potatoes had helped to sustain and organize an extended pretend episode.

Exploration and imitation are still an essential part of the learning process for older children and adults. However, there is a different mental orientation. As adults we can explore the world by reading a book or imitate another person's skill by following instructions. We can avoid much of the external repetition involved in exploration and imitation by repeating new ideas mentally and by imagining ourselves in different situations. We can systematically compare present and past experiences because more of our experience has been stored in highly retrievable symbols. Most importantly, we have developed logical tests to refine and evaluate symbolic ideas. This orientation toward the creation and control of symbols, whether they be key words, pictures, or combinations of sound and motion, is the hallmark of conceptual thinking.

Preschool children are in a transition period between the action-oriented world view of infants and toddlers and the thought-oriented view of older children and adults. Imaginative play spans these two world views. On the one hand, it is based on imitation and exploration, the major characteristics of sensory motor intelligence. On the other hand, it involves the abstraction, sequencing, categorization, and generalization of symbols. Imaginative play is imitation and exploration cast into a symbolic mold.

Because it is a bridge between sensory motor learning and symbolic thinking, imaginative play necessarily involves constant exploration of the relationship between action and thought. Pretending consists of actions that mimic reality, yet these actions are more like thoughts, flexible and reversible, capable of going in one direction one moment and doubling back on themselves the next.

The relationship between thought and action has been a subject of philosophical debate for centuries. Although we cannot be definitive about this relationship, we can be certain that there is a difference between dreaming of a car accident and actually having one. There is a difference between imagining that a make-believe villain has been killed and a person really dying. This is the kind of distinction that preschool children have difficulty making because they are just beginning to realize that thought and action represent different planes of reality. Their confusion over the relationship between thought and action is reflected in imaginative play.

One sign of this confusion is that preschool children tend to overreact to contradiction in a pretend situation. Zach, for example, got mad at his mother for suggesting they sit down and wait for a streetcar on the moon. It was an innocent enough suggestion, prompted by the fact that she was tired of pretending to walk on the moon with Zach. "There are no streetcars on the moon," he snapped. In this instance, Zach had lost the perspective that they were engaged in a pretend situation where any kind of ride is possible.

An even clearer example occurred one day when Scott was watching a football game with his father. Scott's habit was to pretend to kick a football whenever his favorite team, the Denver Broncos, kicked the ball. On this particular occasion Scott pretended to kick a field goal as the same event took place on the field. His father teased him by putting his hand up and saying, "I blocked your kick that time." Scott tried to argue with him, but when his father did not apologize, Scott became very upset and said he would not play with him anymore. For the rest of the game, he pretended to kick the ball away from his father. Although his father's teasing was only a thought, Scott treated it like a real action.

Another sign that preschool children often regard pretending as being real is the use of magical rituals. The children act as if a pretense will not be sufficiently real unless a ritualistic set of actions is performed. The clearest examples are ritualistic phrases. Jad used such a phrase whenever he was engaged in a pretend activity that involved physical strength and agility. Reaching back like a javelin thrower, and with a most determined look on his face, he instructed his *Star Wars* sword, "Born Arrow, make your second marks." Then he let fly, throwing the sword as far as he could at an imaginary Darth Vader. Going down the slide he cried out, "Dive into second place." A solitary game of pretend basketball produced a running commentary:

"Go—hike. Make your second marks. I try to make second base. Get your going. I have to do ten second teams."

Apparently, all this magical gibberish stemmed from footraces around the backyard that his father timed with a stopwatch. He usually told Jad, "Take your mark, get set—go," and Jad had concluded that such phrases were necessary for the success of any athletic endeavor.

Another bit of evidence that indicates preschool children are mixed up about the power of pretend ideas is their unwillingness to take the part of a bad character. Older children relish the part of a robber or a witch, but preschool children act as if taking such a part might really lead to bad consequences. Jennifer was holding her own with a group of older children until one child suggested that Jennifer be the monster. The age differential became immediately apparent. "I don't want to be the monster," Jennifer whined, rushing to the security of her mother's arms.

In a similar way, a fearful event within a pretend episode can upset the delicate balance between reality and fantasy, making fantasy too real to be acceptable. Marcus, for example, enjoyed pretending that a tiny cowboy figure whose head was missing was dead. In fact, all the cowboy figures were buried under a plastic cup. But when it was time to pick up the toys, Marcus did not want to touch these dead cowboys. They remained in their plastic grave.

Although we have described a number of examples in which children were mixed up over the difference between pretend and real, confusion is the exception rather than the rule. Most of the time preschool children are aware they are pretending, even if they take the pretending more seriously than adults. Pretending may be closer to reality for the children than it is for adults, but they still know the difference. The behavior of the children changes in a pretend situation. They imitate real actions without expecting the normal results. For example, they blow out birthday candles without expecting the candles to be first lit and then extinguished. They accept substitute objects, such as a doll for a baby or a toy car for a real one. They exaggerate the normal sounds and movements associated with an event, like making loud eating noises while pretending to eat and seeming to throw huge handsful of food into their mouths.

The surest sign that preschool children are making good progress in separating real action from pretend action is the use of verbal clues. When a child renames an object, such as calling a block of wood a piece of cake, it indicates a pretend orientation. Pretending is even more clearly indicated when a child reassigns normal roles, "I be Mommy and you be me." The most powerful words for elucidating the nature of a situation are words like "real" and "pretend." Children who hear these words in context will pick them up easily because they are so useful. When Jennifer's mother asked if Jennifer wanted to help cook dinner, she responded, "I just want to do the pretend cooking." Kori, who was pretending that her doll Alyse had her own doll, commented, "Isn't that silly? Alyse gave her doll real water."

Older preschool children may make a special effort to point out that pretending is not real, as if they were worried that adults might misjudge their intelligence. Kristine became very intent when she showed us how to check her doll's heart with a stethoscope. Yet she was quick to add, "She doesn't have a real heart—the heart doesn't sound like anything." Later she took the doll's blood pressure and reiterated the pretend nature of her examination, "Now the blood pressure—she really doesn't have any."

When preschool children become able to talk about real and pretend in this way, it does not mean that they always understand the

Dr. Kristine

difference between fantasy and reality. But it does suggest that they understand the difference at least some of the time. Moreover, the door is opened for more sophisticated discussions. Adults have opportunities to explain how television is a form of pretending, how dreams are like pretending, how teasing is related to pretending, and how wishes are similar to pretending.

SELECTING KEY ACTIONS

Not surprisingly, the first and most persistent role that young children assume is the role of parent. By the age of two, children have begun to form a notion about the key actions of a parent. They have abstracted out the idea that parents, above all else, take care of children and babies. This caretaking may entail a host of tasks such as cooking, feeding, cleaning, washing, giving baths, or putting children to bed. It can also include emotional behaviors like hugging, kissing, and comforting. Each child abstracts out his own blend of these parent behaviors. We can see the process more clearly by looking at some examples.

When visiting Jennifer's house one day, she invited us to dinner in her room. She served us pretend roast beef and potatoes, which she cautioned us about eating because it was too hot. She sat at a little table with us and busied herself pouring us drinks and urging us to have second helpings. Then she brought out brownies hot from the oven for dessert. As we finished our pretend eating, Jennifer cleared the dishes to wash them at the oven, which also doubled as sink and refrigerator. When we asked Jennifer why she didn't serve herself some dinner she looked a bit puzzled. For Jennifer the parent role involved cooking and serving the food, but not eating it.

In Judy's case the action of cleansing was abstracted as the most significant behavior of a parent. Judy acted out the parent role with a favorite doll which had a rag body and a washable face. She kept the doll's face spotlessly clean, but in time the rag body became dirty. Judy begged her mother to take the doll apart and wash it. When her mother explained that it was impossible, Judy tried to talk Grandma into washing it. By now the doll was called "Dirty Gerty" by everyone. Judy became depressed and so her mother bought an identical doll and christened it Clean Jean. Judy resisted the new doll for several weeks, but eventually Jean was granted the privilege of going to bed with Judy. Now Clean Jean also goes shopping with Judy at the mall, but before they leave Judy wraps Jean in a towel to keep her in pristine condition. Dirty Gerty, who is still around, stays on the floor. Judy occasionally picks her up, gives her a kiss and says, "Dirty Gerty was left all alone, but she's all right." Judy seems to care for poor Gerty, but something is lacking in their relationship. Unless Judy can keep her babies clean, she cannot play out the role of parent to her own satisfaction.

Jamie placed special emphasis on the parent as a runner of errands, as the one who goes out and gets the essentials for daily living. The routine was always the same. Jamie put on a pair of old sunglasses and jumped into his red "wheeling" car. He pretended to shut the door and turn on the ignition. Making appropriate "Varroomm, varroomm" sounds, he drove down the hall. At the far end of the hall, Jamie parked the car, hung up his keys on an invisible hook, and took off his sunglasses. The needed items, such as milk and a newspaper for daddy, were always conveniently located in a particular spot on the wall. Then, donning his sunglasses and starting up his engine, Jamie drove home and delivered his purchases.

Each of these children played out the role of a nurturing parent, but in each case a different action had been abstracted as being most important. The same process occurs when children adopt an occupational role like doctor or teacher. With each patient the pretend doctor goes through a set of essential actions, whether it involves listening to the heart, dispensing pills, or giving a shot. In the same way the role of a teacher is established by asking questions about the alphabet, telling imaginary pupils to be quiet and pay attention, or some other stereotypical behavior.

When preschool children become interested in superhero roles, the key action is often a gesture. Tarzan beats on his chest or the Hulk breaks out of his shirt. The gesture may be an auditory one, like the siren noises that pretend firemen and policemen always seem to make, or the cry of "Superman" as a child leaps to the rescue. John, for example, had abstracted the action of kicking as the essence of super-power. When his Superman doll attacked the dragon inside the living room lamp, he kicked in the door of the dragon's house. When John marched his farm animals into the barn, the horse began to kick down the door, yelling, "Let me out, let me out." In John's mind kicking was a symbol of great strength.

At times children will attempt to abstract out the actions of a role that they do not know very well, and the result may be unexpected and comical. After seeing a picture of a telephone repair truck in a book, Erik decided to become a telephone repairman. For several weeks he knocked on the doors of neighbors asking them if they needed their phone fixed. When he found a willing customer, he entered the house and looked at the telephone. "Problem with the wires," he would mumble as he knowingly looked up at the ceiling. Next Erik would take

"Let me out! Let me out!"

out his wooden mallet and tap on the wall. In no time the wires were fixed and he went on his way.

Although Erik had never seen a real telephone repairman, he had abstracted the accurate but amusing fact that people often act like they are destroying something when they are fixing it. They hammer, poke, and tear apart objects in order to fix them. Chad made a similar mistake when playing shoe salesman. Despite some personal experiences with the role, he did not fully understand it. First Chad pretended to measure his mother's foot. Then, after an appropriate pause, he selected a shoe from her closet. "No, these don't fit, better get something else." He tried other shoes, but no, they did not fit any better. In Chad's mind the shoe salesman was a man who went into the back room and came out with shoes that didn't fit—an accurate distillation of real experience, but a misconception of the true role.

There are instances in which children focus on an event more than a particular role. Probably the most common example is the birthday party. Regardless of whose birthday is being celebrated, the most important action is lighting and then blowing out the candles. We watched Heather provide a striking example of this idea.

Like many children she had created a cake from a pegboard. Her pegboard had 100 holes, and she carefully set out to fill every one. Part way through the pegs spilled on the floor, and Heather, in a polite tone, requested help from her mother. "Give me your hand, please." Her

Heather blowing out her birthday cake.

mother finished putting the 100 candles in place, and the cake was ready for lighting. "I need a red one," Heather said as she searched for a red peg that could serve as a match. Having found the appropriate peg, she began systematically to light each row of candles, touching the tip of the red peg to each candle. Heather succeeded in lighting the first few rows, but when she tried to light the middle rows, she kept losing her place. She found herself lighting and relighting the same outside rows. "Please help me light the candles," she requested in frustration. Finally, with her mother's help the monumental job was completed, and the cake was set down in front of her doll, Bessy. It turned out that Bessy was celebrating only her fourth birthday. Nevertheless, Heather helped her blow out all 100 candles, whereupon Bessy, who had been propped up in a sitting position, lost her balance and toppled face first into the cake. Even Heather, who considered the party to be serious business, had to giggle at this unforeseen turn of events.

We saw another typical example of abstracting an action from an important event when we visited Jamie's home. Jamie wanted to play school and solicited our help in constructing a school out of blocks. He painstakingly loaded a miniature vehicle with small doll characters and included a small dog and a rubber ball that wanted to go to school too. Next, he started up the engine by touching the hood of the bus. The highlight of the trip was stopping at a small cardboard stoplight. "Light's red—stop! Light's green—go!" Jamie pretended as he pushed the bus

Jamie loading the school bus.

toward the school. "What happens when everybody gets to school?" Jamie's mother asked. "It didn't start yet," was the reply and the bus circled slowly around the room once more.

Finally, the bus arrived at the school, and Jamie transferred the children to a hole/window we had built in the school. There was not enough room for everyone so Jamie decided that the dog and the ball would have to wait in the bus. He consoled the dog by telling him that he could be the bus driver and listen to a tape on the tape deck. The ball sat beside the dog and listened too. When Jamie's mother asked rather skeptically if the ball had ears, Jamie pointed to a slight bump on the ball. Soon afterward the pretend theme faded, and Jamie lost interest. Nothing really had happened in the school—all the action had taken place in the bus. The critical part of going to school, from Jamie's point of view, was traveling back and forth in the bus.

Young children also abstract salient actions from new experiences. Wendy, for example, took a trip to New York to attend a wedding. When she came home she acted out this theme by pretending to lift her veil, cut the cake, and dance around in a circle. These were the actions of the bride that she had picked out of the whole event. Chad abstracted even less from an evening at a fancy restaurant. "Let's pretend we are drinking wine—let's have a toast," he told his mother several days later. With one action he was able to evoke the larger pretend event of eating at a fancy restaurant.

Whether we look at a child's pretending in terms of a role or an

40

event, certain key actions stand out. These actions are the symbols that establish the pretend role or event and set the stage for more elaborate pretending. Abstracting out key actions is only one part of developing a pretend vocabulary, however. The other side of the coin is abstracting out the most significant objects for pretending. When Jennifer took over the role of cook in the kitchen play we saw this process of abstraction at work. She had abstracted the importance of kitchen appliances, and her all-purpose stove-refrigerator-sink could make things hot, cold, or clean. Jamie had identified keys and sunglasses as necessary for running errands, and road signs were important object symbols for setting up a school. Heather's birthday party was dependent on the pegboard cake, the peg candles, and the peg match. Let us look more closely at this process of selecting object symbols or props.

SELECTING KEY PROPS

Often the critical prop for acting out the role is some sort of costume. Again we see the process of abstraction at work. Heather became her mother one evening by putting on her mother's nightgown, bathrobe, and slippers. Erik pretended to be a businessman by wearing a sport coat that drooped down to his knees. In many cases the most critical part of a costume is the hat. The farmer's costume is a straw hat. The costume for a bride is a veil. On our visit to Jad's home we watched him change hats in order to change his roles. First he put on his cowboy hat and was a singing cowboy, standing on the hood of the family car. Then

Jad as singing cowboy.

he changed to his *Star Wars* helmet. With one hand Jad propped up the oversize helmet so that he could see out the visor; with the other hand he waved a sword at his enemy, Darth Vader.

There are many other instances of critical objects being abstracted for a role or event. The police officer has a gun, Superman has a cape, and the doctor has a needle for giving shots. Here are three of the many interesting examples we observed.

Jeremy was playing a solitary game with two toy cars. The critical prop was a road map. Jeremy drove the two cars along the lines on the map. "You go to the airport, you go to the motel." Eventually the cars crashed and Jeremy admonished them, "See, you didn't do what I told you to." Although the trip seemed to end in disaster, the map beckoned the two cars back on the road and the pretend traveling continued.

Brett had identified a rope as a critical prop for playing out super-hero themes. He used the rope to make a spider web in his room, winding the rope around and between the doorknob, the bedpost, and his desk. Brett's mother pretended to get caught in the web, and Brett rescued her. In another version, Brett tied himself to the clothesline post and had to be rescued by Superman. Brett even "rescued" his baby brother who had just learned to walk, by leading him around with the rope.

Wendy liked to play "visiting" with some neighbor friends. She pretended to be her mother, and the friends pretended to be visitors. The essential props for this theme were a welcome mat and a coffee maker. Outside the door of her room Wendy laid a cloth or blanket to serve as the welcome mat, while inside her room the knob of a dresser became the button and spout of a coffee maker. It seemed to us that Wendy's feeling of hospitality was evident in her choice of these symbolic objects.

The selection of key props is very much influenced by what is at hand. The zoo theme provides a good example. The critical props are wild animals, which are not readily available in most homes. Ken and Jill solved this problem by pretending that the animals on their wallpaper were animals at the zoo. Leroy and Patty used the three little dogs in the backyard as their zoo animals. Of course, there are disadvantages in being limited to the immediate environment. The dog that Leroy and Patty selected to be a fierce cheetah was so content that he would not even eat the cookies they tried to feed him.

When a critical object needs to be especially large, it is almost essential to use whatever is handy. Laura and her mother wanted to take the elevator to another floor when they were on a pretend shopping trip. The closet worked admirably. Ken and Jill used a closet in their room as a helicopter. Zach and his grandfather took trips to the moon in a closet that was a rocket ship. Other large objects like beds, showers, and card tables were used as key props in similar ways.

In describing the abstraction of objects for pretending, we have glossed over differences in realism. A prop may be quite realistic, like the nightgown Heather wore when she was playing mother. A prop may look more or less real, but be a toy, such as the toy cars Jeremy was driving on the map. Or, a prop may look pretty unrealistic but share some attribute with the real object it symbolizes, like the knob that Wendy used for a coffee-maker. This last category of props is particularly interesting because it involves a second level of abstraction. The child abstracts out the kind of object he needs, and then he abstracts out a critical attribute of that object.

This second level of abstraction can be seen when a child converts a favorite toy into a versatile prop. Chad's favorite possession was a crane. According to his parents, Chad used his crane for a variety of props, including a movie projector and a gas pump with hose. In each case, the crane had some characteristics that suggested the imaginary prop. The string and hook of the crane were like the hose of a gas pump, the wheel that turned the wrench was like the reel of a movie projector, etc. Dale's use of his favorite fire engine provides an even clearer example. Dale pretended that his fire engine was a hedge trimmer, a chain saw, and an outboard motor. Although these seem like strange uses for a truck, the extended ladder of the fire engine did look

David trimming the hedge.

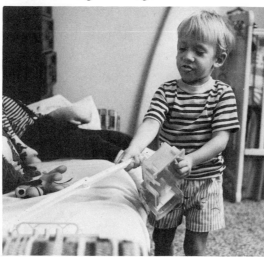

like the blade of a chain saw or the propeller of an outboard motor.

Often we cannot be sure whether a child has decided first that he needs a certain prop and then found an appropriate object, or has found the object first and then decided that it would make a good prop. Most props are selected to some extent because they are handy or because they have intrinsic appeal. At the same time most props make sense in the pretend context. They look right. Whatever the initial impetus for the selection of a prop, it is truly amazing how young children look around them and see a world full of imaginary props. Most of us would see nothing remarkable in a long wire brush. To Jennifer it was an ear of corn that could be cooked on the grill. We would be more attracted to a baby toy with brightly colored balls sticking out in different directions. But few of us would have Jennifer's insight that it would make a marvelous bubble gum dispenser.

We have been talking about the selection of props as though it always involved choosing objects that already exist. Preschool children also are able, and very willing, to make their own key props. We have already described the 100-candle cake that Heather was making with her pegboard. Materials like pegs, Tinkertoys, and wooden beads are ideal for making small props: lollipops, ice cream cones, guns and flagpoles. Other props can be created out of clay or playdough. Blocks can be used to make buildings that are critical for a particular theme, or larger props can be constructed with furniture and blankets.

A particularly interesting way of making a key prop is to turn into

Jennifer cooking her ear of corn.

one yourself. Terry became a vigorous train engine. Rotating his arms like wheels he announced. I'm a train, hop on me. Everyone hop on." Zach pretended to throw a pie on the floor. Then, throwing himself on the floor, he announced that he was a vacuum cleaner. He made exaggerated sucking sounds as he pretended to clean up the mess. Chad even decided to be a sink at the doctor's office. "The water comes out of my mouth," he explained to his mother. "How do I turn you on?" she asked. "Use my ears," he replied. "My right ear is for hot water and my other ear is for cold."

There are times when children do not seem to be using any props at all in their pretending. Several families reported that their children enjoyed acting out a ball game without using a ball. Scott and Brandon followed a picnic lunch with a no-ball throw and catch routine. The pretend game of catch saved them from the trouble of chasing after missed balls, thereby speeding up the game and increasing the fun. In time they even developed rules for playing pretend baseball and football.

Invisible props are common when a pretend game evolves into wild, exaggerated humor. Erik started such a game one day in the car. "There's a bus in my ear," he told his father. His father feigned surprise, leaned over, and looked into Erik's ear. Then he pretended to reach into Erik's ear, grabbed the bus, and threw it out the car window, saying indignantly, "Get out of Erik's ear." Not so sure that he wanted to lose the bus, Erik yelled, "I want to see it." His father reached back out the window and said, "Come back here bus," whereupon Erik ate the offending vehicle. The game continued in this fashion for some time as Erik thought up other unlikely intruders that might be in his ear.

Some children actually develop a style of using invisible props. As we described earlier, Jamie found everything he needed on his shopping trips by pretending to reach into the wall. On another occasion, Jamie was playing postman in the hospital lobby while waiting for his mother to give birth. The wall served as his post office and he pulled out a letter or package for everyone in the lobby. On still another occasion, Jamie pulled a telephone out of his uncle's leg.

When children use invisible props in this way, we still see the process of object selection going on. The ball obviously was a critical prop for Scott and Brandon's sports events, the oversized vehicles were necessary to establish the absurdity of Erik's ear game. Although invisible props may not be seen, their presence certainly is felt. Like the selection of visible props, they are part of a child's growing vocabulary of symbolic objects.

EXPRESSING IDEAS IN THE VOCABULARY OF PRETENDING

In this final part of the chapter we want to look at ways in which a child's vocabulary of pretend symbols is used to express more elaborate themes. Returning for a moment to our analogy between language and pretending, we can think of a symbol as being more like a word, while a theme is more like a sentence, or perhaps a short story.

When children learn to talk, they usually go through a single word stage. During this period the children consolidate their vocabularies through repetition. They label favorite objects and pictures over and over again. Presumably the repetition helps solidify their memory of each word, and in time this consolidation paves the way for expansion. At first, a new word is used rather mechanically in a restricted context. After a while the word becomes more familiar and is used in a variety of situations.

Much the same thing seems to happen in pretending. The link between the vocabulary of pretend symbols and more elaborate pretend themes is repetition and consolidation. Small bits of pretend play are repeatedly played out with the same key actions and key props. This repetition, like the repetition of labels by a toddler, serves as an external form of memorization. Each replay helps cement that pretend idea in memory so that it can be retrieved and played out next time with greater ease. In time new details are added. Consolidation of a pretend vocabulary leads to greater elaboration, just as consolidation of a word vocabulary leads to sentences. As one version of a pretend idea is mastered through repetition, the possibility of a more elaborate version opens up. Then that version is consolidated, until it too is elaborated.

We will look at how this spiral process works by describing three closely related kinds of elaborated pretending. First, pretending can be extended into longer and richer sequences. More events or steps can be added. Second, pretending can be enriched by greater organization of props, by categorizing and collecting sets of symbolic objects. Finally, pretending can be elaborated by playing out a theme in more than one setting. We have labeled these three kinds of elaborated pretending as (1) filling in the plot, (2) organizing the set, and (3) generalizing the theme.

FILLING IN THE PLOT

There is a great deal of ritualistic repetition in the pretend themes of young children, and the rate of change is slow. Usually it takes a period of weeks for a theme to grow noticeably longer and more complex. In Laura's case the theme of a tea party was consolidated and expanded over a four-month period. The record of these tea parties provides a detailed example of how a plot is filled in.

The main event at a tea party is the serving of drinks, and as anyone who attends a child's tea party soon finds out, tea is only one of many possible refreshments. At various times Laura offered tea, grape drink, apple juice, orange juice, chocolate milk, and fresh water. At one of the first tea parties in our record, Laura included a real plum as an additional prop. She pretended the plum was an egg and said, "A chick will pop out." Soon, however, the skill involved in handling a knife became the focus of the party:

> "I'm cutting my plum. The characters (miniature "Sesame Street" characters) are watching me cut just like Mommy and Daddy . . ."

The next tea party scene occurred when Laura and her mother were pretending to have lunch at the mall. Laura wanted another plum to cut but settled for an apple. Shortly after that her attention was switched to a new manipulative skill. Cheerios were served at the luncheon tea parties, and they were eaten by fitting a separate Cheerio on each prong of a fork.

These initial additions appeared because they were manipulative challenges. It took skill for Laura to cut the fruit or to impale the Cheerios. Although these details seemed to drop out after a few weeks, they had served a purpose. Laura was tuned into the idea that food could be served along with the drinks. At the next tea party she cooked a roast, and the plum showed up in a new form: "I want something to go with the roast. I'll make a pie—plum pie."

"I'm cutting my plum."

Like many preschool children, Laura started by identifying the meat and the dessert as the elements in a good meal. Her cooking quickly expanded. Pot roast and pie continued to be staple items, but she also tried other combinations such as pea soup and coffee-chocolate cake and peanut butter-French toast, eggs and cream of wheat-mushroom soup and tossed salad. One day she even cooked a separate color of ice cream for each person at the tea party. There was red, yellow, blue, and black ice cream.

About the time that Laura's cooking expanded she added other details too. The dishes for the tea party were set on a large pillow, and a booster seat was provided for Laura's favorite doll. Although Laura and her mother drank tea with the dolls, the tea party was fast becoming a formal dinner.

> "This is a little dinner" (drinking the tea). "Next time (in a minute) we will have more dinner—roast beef and dessert. Would you like dinner music and a candle? I'll turn the music and TV on."

Just as the preparation for the meal had become more elaborate, so had the cleanup operation. In the beginning Laura was content to stack the dishes after the tea party. Now she used a cabinet knob as a faucet and washed the dishes. In keeping with her preference for realistic props, Laura went to the closet and found a towel for drying the dishes.

Several weeks later the tea party theme took a new twist. The food was packed and Laura pretended to go to the beach. True to form the company ate roast beef. However, the idea of having a tea party at the beach did not really catch on. There were so many other things to do at the beach, like getting a suntan, drying off after swimming, and reading a book.

At the last tea party in our record, Laura had returned to the formal dinner, but she had found a new way to incorporate the beach idea. She brought a quilt and a fishing pole into the family room. The quilt became the water and Laura proceeded to catch a fish. She got out her pots and pans and cooked the fish with sauce. "Be careful of the steam," she warned the dolls. Then she arranged her dishes on the pillow and made a candle by putting a block on a coaster. She served her dolls fish, broccoli, and sandwiches. (There was still a hint of the beach picnic.) After dinner she washed the dishes under the cabinet knob, dried them with a towel, and blew out the candle. Laura's mother did not report the presence of any tea at all in this last tea party. Serving drinks had declined from being the central event to being a detail not important enough to notice.

Laura's tea party theme evolved slowly as Laura and her mother thought up new ideas. Sometimes a plot is filled in more quickly when a child combines smaller routines that are already well established. A good example is Jennifer's picnic theme, which was her favorite activity with Nana.

The scene begins with Jennifer and Nana putting a picnic basket and other props in their car. The car is made out of a small chest (the dashboard), an inflated life preserver (the steering wheel), and a low stool. Jennifer drives the car, and after arriving at the beach, the picnic basket is opened and the table set. Jennifer cooks and serves hot clam chowder from a thermos bottle, along with peanut butter sandwiches. Nana also receives hot coffee and a handful of cookies. After they eat, Jennifer tells Nana to build a sand castle. Often it rains at this point, and Nana is required to hold a miniature umbrella. Occasionally Nana and Jennifer go swimming. Throughout this beach play Jennifer announces periodically that it is time to eat more soup, and eventually, when the soup runs out, the picnic ends.

The initial inspiration for this theme was a real picnic, but the main reason for the theme's success was that Jennifer already had learned to play out several key parts of the sequence. Earlier we mentioned Jennifer's interest in being the cook and the server. Like Laura, she had experimented with a variety of menus, and it was easy for her to be the cook and server on a picnic. Months earlier Jennifer and Nana had pretended to shop with Jennifer's toy shopping cart. They had developed a routine for shopping for clam chowder. When Jennifer decided to cook and serve hot soup at the picnic, it was inevitable that it would be clam chowder.

It also was easy for Jennifer to drive the car to the beach because she had already developed considerable skill as a pretend driver. Jennifer and her mother commute twenty-five miles to work several days a week, and all this driving had made an impression. At home Jennifer constantly pretended to drive. At first she simply steered, then she added details like stopping for a red light, putting on the turn signal and wipers, and paying the toll booth operator. With her knack for finding props Jennifer saw potential cars everywhere. She found a basket in the laundry room and scooted around the floor. In the dining room she propped herself on the window seat and made a "vrroomm, vrroomm" sound. Jennifer even saw possibilities in a pole lamp.

Pretending to swim was another bit that had been played out separately and could be added to the picnic theme. Of course, Nana was needed, especially the first few times, to keep the play moving from one event to another. Even after many picnics there were signs that this elaborated theme was a patchwork of smaller routines. For example,

Jennifer had forgotten to bring salt and pepper on one of the first picnics and then had to run back to the closet to get it, even though she was supposed to be on the beach. She continued to reenact this mistake on subsequent picnics, and it became an illogical subunit in the whole event. When it came to building the sand castle, which was not a preexisting routine, Jennifer did not take a direct part. Instead, she supervised Nana's efforts. Probably because Jennifer was not involved in this sand castle building, she kept cooking and serving more soup. As the play lost meaning to her, she reverted to a routine she understood— cooking and serving.

As children fill in an imaginary plot, they are learning to sequence information, to create a series of events that makes sense. The structure of real experience becomes illuminated as it is projected into an imaginary world. As a result of her elaborated tea parties, Laura understood on a deeper level the order that is implicit in cooking and serving a meal. At the same time the process of filling in the plot helps children appreciate their power to create structure through sequencing. The sequence of imaginary events may be rigid and somewhat arbitrary, as it was in Jennifer's picnic routine, but the children are beginning to consider the causal and logical relationships between these events.

ORGANIZING THE SET

Earlier we discussed how the identification of key props enriches the playing out of a pretend role. In the same way a collection of props can complement the expansion of a pretend theme. We have already alluded to these collections in describing how Laura and Jennifer expanded their favorite themes. Laura's props varied somewhat from one tea party to the next, but the most important ones were the pillow that became a tablecloth, the candle, the knob for washing dishes, the towel for drying the dishes, and the dishes themselves. Jennifer's picnic theme depended on a brown thermos, a red-and-white tablecloth, certain dishes with a teddy bear painted on them, and a tiny umbrella that had been a table decoration. These collections of props had a direct effect in stimulating a more elaborate sequence of events.

The same kind of effect can be seen in the doctor play of preschool children. Doctor play is invariably dominated by the props. Children love to tap all over a person's body if a doctor's hammer is available. They will cover a patient with Band-Aids if given the opportunity. Because the children want to keep handling the props, their patients never seem to get any better. An example from Laura's doctor play will illustrate. First she put on her nurse's uniform, a green nightgown and a paper hat, and announced, "Yes, I'm going to zamen the dolls." After taking each doll's temperature and giving each one a shot, they were laid in their beds, which were trays the family had been using for dinner. Laura gave each doll some aspirin, but one of the dolls was still sick. The nurse put her stethoscope on the doll's stomach:

> "My dolly is sick, so I'm nursing her. Her stomach is aching. I nurse her. Watch me."

The doll was given another drink of medicine and her eyes were checked with an eye chart. "Is dolly better?" asked Laura's mother. "No, she's still sick," Laura answered, and she gave the doll another spoonful of medicine, this time using her own saliva for the medicine.

Although a collection of props can stimulate a greater variety of pretend actions, sometimes the collection and arrangement of props is a substitute for action. When children do not understand the actions involved, they may put most of their energy into organizing the pretend set. Chad's father had an office in their home. It was predictable that Chad would try to express this theme in his imaginative play. Not understanding the meaning of all the paper work and telephone calls, however, he concentrated on creating his own office environment. His office needed to be private, like his father's, so Chad selected a closet. A footstool in front of the closet represented his desk. Chad sat inside the closet on a small barrel with his office equipment around him: a basket for outgoing mail, a toy telephone, and a pad and pencil. Although Chad imitated his father by talking on the phone and writing on the pad, the major avenue for elaborating this theme lay in the collection and arrangement of props.

Shortly before the study ended Chad's mother called us and reported that Chad had built a spaceship in his room. When we arrived we discovered that the spaceship, which was in one corner of the room, resembled a high technology office. Chad had carefully arranged the following items on top of his toy chest: a cash register, a phone with a switchboard, a toy typewriter, a toy piano keyboard, and a flashlight case that served as a "talker thing" (a microphone/dictaphone). Chad was too shy to show us how the spaceship worked. In private he probably pushed the buttons and talked into the flashlight, but we left with the impression that most of his time was spent organizing this pretend environment.

Chad's spaceship seemed to us to be a kind of office, but it also illustrates another theme that leads to prop collection, the theme of taking a trip. Preschool children get so engrossed in selecting items for a trip and packing them in a suitcase, that often the plot stops there. It is not clear what kind of actions should occur on the trip, and so the imaginative play focuses on the process of packing up.

Laura took several typical pretend trips to the beach. On one occasion the miniature characters accompanied her. Laura brought along doll dresses for their beach towels and extra covers to keep them warm. She packed a lunch and brought a hair dryer for their wet hair. She included some suntan cream, but she was still not satisfied. "They need more supplies at the beach—they need a carousel." A wheel was found that could serve the purpose. In the end, Snoopy, Bert, Ernie, Mickey, and a baby were laid face-down on their towels, with the rest of the props arranged around them. Laura declared by way of a finale, "Everyone is sleepy." Laura was not interested in making anything else happen at the beach. The elaboration had come in the preparation.

As we imagine Snoopy and his friends being placed carefully on separate doll dresses, we can see that organizing the set has an aesthetic dimension. Preschool children try to lay out a set of props so that it looks and feels right. Given a set of toy furniture they will spend hours arranging it, moving it, arranging it again. Some unorthodox arrangements may appear, such as a bathroom with three toilets in a row. But that only means that the child thinks such an arrangement makes a bathroom look suitably distinguished.

In the collection and arrangement of props, preschool children like to create logical categories. Wild animals usually are separated from tame ones. Animals on a farm are further subdivided by kind. Other toys may be sorted by size, function, or color. Jennifer, for example, used a set of colored squares to create a garden. The green squares were string beans, the red squares were radishes, and the yellow squares were lemons that pop out of the ground.

The preschool child's interest in categorizing props will eventually grow into an understanding of logical categories, just as the child's recognition of sequence in pretending will lead to an understanding of mathematical sequence. Imaginative play is not the only route to this understanding, but we presume that the elaboration of pretend themes significantly affects the development of logico-mathematical thinking. For preschool children, however, the main thrust in collecting and organizing props is not governed by considerations of logic. The intent is to create a sensible environment. What goes with what, and how this pretend environment can be made pleasing to the eye and the heart—these are the primary considerations in organizing a set for imaginative play.

GENERALIZING THE THEME

The final kind of elaborated pretending to be discussed is the process of generalizing a pretend idea. One way to generalize a theme is to repeat the same set of actions with each of the characters in a scene. In this case, the child is following the principle that whatever is good for one character is good for the next one as well. Here are two examples from the pretending of Jennifer, who frequently generalized her themes in this way.

One day Jennifer accompanied her mother to the obstetrician. She was worried about the doctor listening to her mother's stomach with a stethoscope. Later at home, Jennifer's parents showed her how to listen herself, and she began to understand that there was a baby inside her mother and that it would come out someday. Jennifer demonstrated her understanding by pretending to be the obstetrician. "Time for a checkup," she told her dolls and stuffed animals as she lined them up. She put the stethoscope on the stomach of the first doll and said, "Shirley, you have a baby Shirley in your tummy—the baby's going to come out of your tummy." Pooh Bear had a baby Pooh in his tummy; Curious George had a baby George; Raggedy Ann had a baby Raggie, and so on through the entire cast of characters. The idea of having a baby was generalized to anyone with a stomach.

At school Jennifer was concerned about wetting the cot during naptime. She also realized that being able to take care of yourself in the bathroom at school was considered a sign of being grown-up, and she did not want to be identified as a baby. Her parents reported that at home she started lining up her miniature doll characters and having each of them go to the bathroom. As tiny as they were, Jennifer made certain that each doll pulled down her imaginary pants, wiped herself, pulled up her pants, and flushed the toilet. At her grandmother's house the same scene was reenacted, this time using regular-sized dolls and an ice bucket for a toilet. Again, the idea of using the toilet properly was generalized to anyone with a bottom.

As these examples make clear, there is a ritualistic dimension to this kind of elaborated pretending. It is essential that every character receive the standard treatment, and if the play is interrupted before the ritual is finished, the children become upset.

This way of generalizing a theme is more typical of younger preschool children. It is a generalization of limited scope in that it reduces all the characters to a common denominator. A more powerful form of generalization occurs when children play out a similar theme in different settings. In this case they are finding a new way to express an old idea, and in the process elaborating the old idea. Wendy played out several roles that involved delivering or picking up something at the door. There was a central hallway in the house with several doors opening off it. Wendy used these doors for her delivery games. In one version she was the Avon lady, who left a catalog at each door. When her mother had time to play too, Wendy would knock on the door and give her sales pitch:

> "Hello. I'm the Avon lady. Here's your book. What would you like? . . . This cream will make your skin nice and soft. . . ."

On other occasions Wendy was a newspaper girl and delivered a newspaper to each door. Sometimes, when her mother was sewing, Wendy put a piece of fabric on her head and pretended it was a Halloween costume. Then holding a paper bag she knocked on the doors in the hall, especially the one in which her mother was sewing, and announced, "Trick or treat!"

Chad had generalized the theme of giving someone else a ride. Sometimes he made a train out of cushions and pretended he was the conductor. A variation involved placing the kitchen chairs against the fireplace. Then he rang a bell and announced:

> "It's a trolley. Is everybody on . . . ? Okay, the ride's over. Everybody off."

Chad pretended to be a taxi driver and took his mother on errands for a fee. After a visit to Disney World he even imagined he could give people a ride on the balloon he had brought back:

> "I'm taking people on a balloon ride.
> There's a basket there where the people sit. Okay, we're going on the ride (and he pulled the balloon around the room)."

A theme may be generalized so strongly that it appears continuously in a child's pretending. David's favorite theme was going on safari. We watched him create the scene. A tent was set up on a throw rug and a rope tied to a nearby door in order to stop wild animals from entering the camp. Then animals were hidden among some pillows and blocks, which formed the jungle. A man was placed in the safari truck and the hunt began. "Sight the gorilla," David instructed the man, whose name was Chief Sayette. Soon a gorilla was found and a fight ensued. The gorilla eventually was subdued, tied up, and put in the truck. Back at the camp the gorilla was transferred to a cage. Later a giraffe was captured

David setting up for a safari.

and placed in a cage beside him. Then the man left on a filming expedition, presumably to catch some more animals on film.

A similar, but life-size, rendition of the safari theme was reenacted several minutes later when David ran outside and jumped on an air mattress located in the swimming pool. "Got to rescue the gorillas," David announced as he paddled himself across the pool using his arms as oars. All of a sudden, David disappeared again and for several minutes we heard nothing. A roaring sound emanating from the tree house broke the silence. "Give up—you're captured. Now eat all your food," David commanded in an authoritative voice.

As we looked at both versions of the safari game it was obvious that chasing and capturing were the critical elements that David had abstracted. In fact, these same elements dominated most of his pretending. A little later we watched David play a pretend game of football in which he dashed through the family room and plucked an imaginary ball from Winter Bear's arms. After that he put on his sheriff outfit and captured his two-year-old sister who was supposed to be a robber. Even the pictures of David on the playground show him chasing one of his schoolmates.

In a similar way Erik generalized the theme of being in a cave. As a two-year-old he was fascinated by stories about animals living in caves, and a favorite storybook character was a boy named Henry who explored caves. Erik would ask his parents to draw pictures of caves with animals peeking out. He learned how to make a primitive cave himself with blocks. Putting his miniature dolls inside a simple enclosure, he announced with satisfaction, "Can't get out."

As a three-year-old, a favorite storybook character was Johnny Lion, who hid in a large box to protect himself from the dripping rain. Erik would say to his parents, "I want to make a dark, dark cave like Johnny Lion," and he would expect them to help him stretch a blanket over a table. Caves became incorporated into pretend games. When Erik's father was sitting down, Erik would step between his legs and say, "Close cave." His father would close his legs tightly so that Erik could not escape. Erik would squeal and twist, but the only words that would release him were "Open cave," which he would pronounce with a great sense of power. When his father was taking a bath, Erik would pretend that the space under his father's knees was a cave into which he would float rubber animals and toy boats.

As a four-year-old, Erik invented his own kind of camper, which was like a cave on wheels. A blanket was draped over two chairs that were back to back. Then Erik's tricycle was parked beside the chairs and the blanket extended over the back part of the tricycle. Erik could pretend to drive wherever he wanted and then camp in the attached cave. He also learned to build a hollow pyramid with large blocks. The pyramid was called a mountain and the inside of the mountain was a cave, which Erik filled with rocks and colored blocks. The miniature dolls, who had been trapped in earlier caves, were now tourists and park rangers who explored the cave and collected crystals and gems.

Just as children naturally try to fill in a plot or organize a set of props, they try to find new ways to express their favorite pretend ideas. Any new concept that intrigues them will start showing up in different pretend scenes. Chad, for example, was intrigued with the concept of "heavy" when we visited his home. The battery of his spaceship was heavy, the toy piano he lifted was heavy, the invisible package he delivered to his mother as the U.P.S. man was heavy. It is common to see preschool children exploring the meaning of new words, like big and little, young and old, tomorrow and yesterday, inside and outside, as they pretend. As our examples illustrate, however, their powers of generalization are also focused on larger patterns. One child generalizes about the kinds of strangers who come to the door, while another explores ways in which a powerful action like driving can be expressed. One child focuses on the excitement of chasing and capturing, while another tries to create a special haven from danger.

We have emphasized in this chapter that imaginative play is an intellectual challenge for young children. Yet the process of creating pretend symbols goes on continually. One child sees camels floating around in the sky. Another child places an "I voted" sticker in the middle of her forehead and calls herself Wonder Woman. As more and more experience is accumulated, each child's metaphors are increasingly linked together to form longer and more complex play episodes. This elaboration of imaginative play is the result of increased skill in abstracting, sequencing, categorizing, and generalizing information.

As the children learn more about the world through pretending, each child is also constructing a unique, personal view of that world. On the one hand, truth is discovered by recreating the real world in imaginative play. On the other hand, truth is discovered by creating a new world in imaginative play. The normal relationships of cause and effect are uncoupled in order to find relationships that are more remote, but valid nonetheless. Kori sings a song after a Tanglewood concert that demonstrates both the intellectual complexity and the creative potential of imaginative play:

> And we woke up after the concert
> and over the night.
> We happened to be birds . . .
> Nightingale birds . . .
> Over the night in Tanglewood.

FROM THE LITERATURE

The effects of imaginative play on intellectual development were studied in a three-year experiment by Eli Saltz, David Dixon, and James Johnson.° Over the three-year period 146 children between the ages of 3.0 and 3.5 years participated. The children, who were predominantly from a lower socioeconomic population, were randomly assigned to small groups. An adult trainer worked with each group fifteen minutes a day, three times a week for approximately six months. Each group was trained according to one of four conditions:

1. Thematic fantasy play—the children acted out fairytales like *The Three Billy Goats Gruff* and *The Three Little Pigs.*
2. Sociodramatic play—the children pretended to reenact real events, such as going to the doctor, shopping at the grocery store, visiting a fire station.

°Eli David Saltz and James Johnson, "Training Disadvantaged Preschoolers on Various Fantasy Activities; Effects on Cognitive Functioning and Impulse Control," *Child Development,* 48 (1977): 367–80.

3. Fantasy discussion—the children listened to fairy tales and answered questions about them.

4. Control condition—the children engaged in activities that did not encourage either fantasy or role-playing, e.g., cutting and pasting, sorting toys into categories, etc.

At the end of each school year the children were tested. I.Q. scores, derived from the Peabody Picture Vocabulary Test and the Picture Test of Intelligence, were significantly higher for the children in the two play conditions. The children in the two play conditions also performed better on the Fantasy Judgment Test by Taylor, in which it is necessary to decide if a picture depicts a realistic or an impossible event. The effects of training on understanding sequential information were less clear. On a test designed by the experimenters, only the more intelligent children in the play conditions were better at telling a story from a series of pictures. When the children were told an illustrated story and then asked to recreate the proper sequence of pictures, there was no difference in performance between the four kinds of groups. The design of the experiment did not allow a direct comparison of the two types of imaginative play, but the data consistently suggested that the thematic fantasy training promoted greater intellectual growth than the condition in which children played out everyday experiences.

Chapter Three

A Way of Feeling
Good About Yourself

All imaginative play, whether the child is being silly or serious, is aimed at creating good feelings. We start this chapter by discussing the kind of pretending that is especially characteristic of intimate friendship—joking around and acting silly. Next, we talk about the good feelings that are a part of replaying a pleasant experience. Thirdly, we talk about the way in which children produce good feelings by assuming the role of a prestigious person. In the fourth section of this chapter, we look more closely at how pretending is used to cope with feelings of fear and anger.

In the world of imaginative play, whether at home, at school, or on the playground, children possess magic power. They become king of the castle, captain of the ship, and commander of the battalions that control outer space. Scary things are overpowered, and exciting things are discovered. Real events that turned out wrong are replayed and revamped. Good feelings are created, bad feelings are overcome, and a stronger sense of identity emerges.

JOKING AROUND AND SILLINESS

Joking around and acting silly is an obvious way of producing good feelings. Adults often encourage young children to be silly for the sheer joy of hearing their delighted laughter and sharing in their fun. As we watch a scene between Zach and his grandfather, it is apparent that both of them are acting silly and having a marvelous time.

Zach is playing in his doghouse (in reality he is hiding under a sheet), and Grandpa is waiting patiently outside. Grandpa's fingers, however, are not behaving very well. They are creeping slowly under the sheet and into the doghouse. Grandpa explains to us, in a most serious tone, that he gets into a lot of trouble because of his fingers, but he can't do anything about them. Just then Zach begins laughing and attacks the fingers. "Ow—Ow," shrieks Grandpa, which makes Zach giggle all the more. "The fingers," he explains quite solemnly to Zach, "just want to see what you're doing."

It is patently absurd to imagine fingers that want to see what is going on, which is precisely why Grandpa's routine produces such joy in Zach. Once the imaginative element is recognized, the strange character of Grandpa's fingers becomes merely ridiculous.

In the same way a mysterious event can be reduced to a playful sham. For example, we watched Wendy's grandmother announce that she would perform the amazing trick of making a penny disappear. Rapidly transferring the penny from one hand to the other, "Nana" eventually presented two tightly closed fists to Wendy. Wendy had no difficulty following the transfers. She immediately pointed to the correct hand, whereupon Nana deftly dropped the penny in her other hand as she opened the fist. Immediately Wendy pointed to the other hand, but again Nana transferred the penny as she opened her hand. Wendy knew the trick, but she wasn't quick enough to catch Nana in the act. The knowledge was sufficient though. Just realizing that it was all a pretense made Wendy giggle in delight. And when her turn came to be the magician, Wendy laughed uproariously as her grandmother pretended to be befuddled by the disappearing penny.

We suspect these examples belong to a set of universal jokes that adults play on young children. All over the world good feelings must arise from the imaginary quality of an amateurish magic trick or a mock attack. Laughter is a strong mortar for cementing the relationship between an adult and a child. Both the adult and the child relish moments of silliness. The tonic of laughter is so invigorating that adults continue to initiate this kind of joking exchange even though the child may exhaust the adult's good humor by insisting on repetition.

For their part, preschool children also try to initiate jokes. Often these jokes consist of adding a silly twist to everyday activities like eating, sleeping, and dressing. Eating is perhaps the most fertile source of ideas. In the first chapter we described the sandwich game at Brett's house where family members became the ingredients in a wiggling, giggling sandwich. This game initially was Brett's idea, and although it is especially creative, it illustrates the general tendency of preschool children to think up eating jokes.

Brian's joke was more typical. After shaping a lump of clay into a patty, he opened his mouth extra wide and pretended to pop it in. "Delicious hamburger," he announced to his classmates. "Think I'll make me another one." Several children followed suit. Melissa and Demetrius both "ate" a clay cookie, Paul bit into a "hot dog" and Tania stuck her head into the bowl of clay insisting it was dog food. Fortunately the teacher intervened before the eating joke got out of hand.

As preschool children grow older, many of their eating jokes go underground and adults are excluded. There are innumerable jokes about eating "poo-poo" and "pee-pee," or whatever other words the child uses. Conventional eating jokes still appear. Brett's mother reported a sophisticated joke that occurred as Brett was playing with some cans in the cupboard. Asked what he was doing, Brett replied, "Making monster soup." "How do you do that?" his mother wondered. Brett gave her the recipe:

Put in cocoa, jelly, green beans, and applesauce—
And one leaf crushed up.

Add two cups of water—
Stir twice—
Then shut in the oven for four hours.

Older preschool children also offer jokes about a variety of other topics. A joke may be presented in a standard form.

Eliza: Now I have a really good riddle. What do you do if your face turns yellow?

Teacher: What?

Eliza: Your hair turns blue.

Eliza: What happens if your hair turns blue?

Teacher: I don't know.

Eliza: Your feet turn yellow. Do you know, you can turn it around, and it's just as funny. Isn't that neat?

The unexpected transformations Eliza imagined were too disconnected to strike her teacher as really funny, but sometimes a joke hits the mark. Karis, for example, developed a regular routine whenever she and her younger sister had finished taking a bath. Before their mother could get their pajamas on them, the two girls would run to a mirror in the hall. Standing there naked before the mirror, Karis would put her arm around her sister and say, "Yes, everybody, this is my sister. Her name is Stacey. I want everyone to meet her." Karis was aware of the incongruity involved in formally introducing a naked person to the rest of the world, and everyone enjoyed the joke.

Laura also created a good joke. "Look," she said to her daddy, holding up a stringy plant. "I'm going to put this spider in your bed." "You're going to do what?" her father asked in mock horror. "Good night," Laura continued, "and don't let the spider bite." Both father and daughter were delighted by the surprising way that Laura directed her father's nightly advice back at him.

Many of the jokes of preschool children are based on word play. Once the children recognize that words are not linked directly with objects, they are able to manipulate words in a playful way. For years adults have been teaching them the names of objects, and now it is time to turn the tables.

Kori's teacher had been teaching her about the properties of a magnifying glass. "You are a magnifying glass," she told her teacher, laughing boisterously at her own joke. In a similar vein, Erik joked with a teacher who was constantly teaching him the names of plants and birds. "This is a pulma," Erik proclaimed, pointing at a mud puddle. "And this is a pulma," Erik went on as he pointed to a nearby tree. After several more examples of pulma, the teacher realized that Erik was not mispronouncing some fancy word—he was simply joking around.

A favorite form of word silliness is to rename members of the family. A child becomes a frog or a rabbit for a day and insists on being referred to as such. In Marcus's family everyone received a new name, and Marcus got the privilege of deciding what it would be. One day they all would be birds, with the literal names of Mommy Bird, Daddy Bird, Four-Year-Old Bird (Marcus) and Toddler Birds (Marcus's twin brothers). On other days their identities became more exotic. Marcus might be referred to as Dorothy, while his mother was the Wizard of Oz, and his brothers, the Scarecrow and the Tin Woodsman.

Between the ages of two and five, the word play of children becomes increasingly sophisticated. More rhyming and alliteration is heard as the children learn to manipulate the separate sounds in a word. Simple puns appear. Eliza liked this riddle-joke, which was going around in her kindergarten class:

> What do you do on Friday? You fry pancakes.
> What do you do on Sunday? You sit in the sun.
> What do you do on Saturday? You just sit.

For a preschool child, playing with words invariably creates good feelings. The words do not have to add up to a hilarious joke. Sometimes the pleasure lies more in the rhythm of the words. The child chants a phrase over and over as an accompaniment to action. "Boomboom, tickle, tickle," Laura chanted as she rocked on her horse. "Scrubble-scrubble, Mr. Bubble-Hubble," she chanted in the bathtub. Other times the pleasure lies in the variety of ideas that flow freely as the child muses to himself. Mandy, while sitting in the sandbox at school, looked at her toes and played with the imaginary ideas that came to mind. Her song conveys the carefree spirit of word play:

> When I take off my shoes, I wiggle them like a worm.
> I really hop in my house like a frog.
> My toes are saying gobble, gobble.
> They are a turkey, like a bunny—see those two little ears.
> This is Mickey Mouse and he wiggles like a worm.
> Mickey Mouse, with his big fat ears, and his face is round.
> And he wiggles like a worm.

REPLAYING PLEASANT TIMES

Joking around, being silly, and playing with words are one way to have a good time through imaginary play. A second way is to play out a happy experience. When something pleasant happens to us, we play it over and over in our minds. By reviewing the experience we are able to savor the pleasure. With children the same kind of reenactment occurs in their imaginative play. Happy events, like a special outing, are re-created day after day.

Chad, for example, frequently began his morning with a trip to McDonalds'. We observed a typical version. Two stuffed friends, Donkey and Kermit the Frog, were placed on a cushion that represented the back seat of Chad's car. "They want to lay down," Chad explained to us. After a few motor noises Chad arrived at his destination and found a parking place, "I think I can park in the back on the grass." Making it clear that he was ordering for a crowd, Chad got out of the pretend car and told his mother, "Give me two hamburgers, four french fries, and six drinks."

Chad and his doll friends all took part in recurrent trips to McDonalds'. At times we see children replaying a happy event by making a doll the central character. After shopping with her mother, Wendy replayed the whole excursion with her favorite doll, Posey. As soon as the shopping excursion was over, Wendy gathered up Posey's wardrobe, and painstakingly changed her outfit. "Oh, Posey," Wendy exclaimed, as she held the doll up to the mirror. "Aren't you a pretty girl. Don't you look nice in your new clothes."

Even an experience that has not been completely pleasant can be transformed through the magic of imaginative play. Good feelings from the experience can be revived, while bad feelings can be suppressed by changing the facts. Mandy's family had run out of gas on the way to Disney World and had waited on the turnpike several hours for assistance. Still, the trip as a whole turned out to be a pleasant experience. When Mandy reenacted this event, she made sure they did not run short of gas. After creating a car by tipping over a chair, she climbed on top and positioned three dolls behind her. "We go to Disney World," she told her dolls. "I start motor, we need gas, we don't run out of gas." And just to make sure, Mandy pretended to drive into a gas station. On the way to Disney World they discussed the rides they would enjoy:

> We're going to see Small World.
> We're going to ride the horses and ride Dumbo.

Mandy also made it clear that some rides would not be repeated on this imaginary trip:

We're not going to Haunted Mansion.
It's too scary.
Those ghosts scare me.

When she decided that they had reached Disney World, Mandy used some blocks to build beds in the motor home. Assured that a bed would be waiting for each of them, Mandy next asked the teacher to help pin identification tags on them so they would not get lost. "We all get our tags on, right?" she said to the dolls. Having covered every contingency that might stand in the way of a good time, Mandy and her friends were ready to set off. "We have to go see Donald Duck and Mickey Mouse," she informed the dolls as they left the classroom.

Whether it is a picnic, a trip to the zoo, or a visit to an ice cream parlor, it is virtually certain that pleasant experiences like these will resurface in imaginative play. Birthdays and special holidays are replayed by almost all children. As we picture Wendy and her friend Jan playing out a Christmas Eve scene, we can see their need to relive the past and to fulfill wishes for the future. "You lie down and go to sleep," Wendy tells Jan. "Now, I'm Santa Claus—no peeking." While Jan pretends to sleep, Wendy gathers books and toys from the room and arranges them around Jan. "Time to wake up. Look what Santa Claus brought you. Merry Christmas." Then it is Jan's turn to be Santa Claus while Wendy is the lucky child. With the help of imaginative play the excitement of Christmas has appeared on an ordinary day.

TAKING ON A POWERFUL ROLE

Another way to produce good feelings through imaginative play is to identify with somebody important and powerful. By taking over the role of a prestigious figure, children endow themselves with instant power and good feelings. The purest example of this effect can be seen when children pretend to be superheroes or monsters. As we discussed in chapter one, there is not a great deal of difference between these two extremes in the minds of preschool children. Both superheroes and monsters share the quality of being all-powerful, and usually the role is not extended beyond a display of strength. Only rarely does a superhero go on to complete the rescue or a monster terrorize his victim. The momentary illusion of power and control is sufficient to provide feelings of intense pleasure.

"Here comes Super Zach!" Zachary announced as he jumped off the slide with an orange towel draped over his shoulders. "Watch out for Frankenstein," Todd screamed out as he knocked down his own block castle. "Hulk is the strongest," Darrius declared as he flexed his

"Watch out for Frankenstein!"

muscles and stuck out his chest. Whether the superhero/monster flies through space, brandishes a sword, flexes his muscles, or lurches into the room with jerky, slow-motion movements, the intent is always the same. "Watch out for me," the child is saying, "I have super strength."

The most elaborated, and certainly the most significant, power role that young children adopt is the role of parent. This is a role nearly all children have experience with, and as we watch them play we can see that they feel good about being in charge. Listen to Terry playing with a dollhouse and a cast of miniature dolls.

"You all have to eat your breakfast first, then you can play . . .
Snoopy, how are you? . . .
Look at this kitchen, it's all messy.
We'd better clean it up."

Terry responds graciously to the mess his children create. He even offers to help clean up. Yet he is clearly the authority figure in the situation. Here is another typical scene, against involving parental authority and eating:

Heather: You be the baby and I'll be Mommy.

Mother: Who's going to be the Daddy?

Heather: I'll be the mommy and daddy, and I'll make tuna fish for supper. But you have to eat baby food.

As these examples illustrate, the parent play of young children combines a nurturing attitude with an authoritarian posture. The children appreciate the fact that parents are both kindly and demanding, both protective and punishing. Mandy captured this paradox quite clearly in some of her pretending:

> "Dolly, you hold real still (while combing Dolly's hair). I don't want to hurt you.
>
> Okay, Dolly, we shampoo your hair. Don't worry, I get soap out of your eye.
>
> I'm sorry, Dolly. I have to spank you for running in the street. It won't hurt you."

Mandy resolved the conflict by pretending that she never really hurt her doll. Even when the doll was spanked, parental authority remained painless. Other children emphasize the punitive side of parent behavior. It is common for adults to overhear children scolding or punishing a doll for some alleged misbehavior. Often the adults react with dismay. Is that how that child's parents really sound? More likely a child who is berating a doll is releasing anger that cannot safely be expressed toward a parent. No matter what the nature of the conflict, a confrontation with a parent leaves a child feeling powerless, and re-enacting the scene in doll play is a way of gaining control and gaining self-confidence.

Most of us have submerged feelings of impotence and frustration that readily come to the surface when we play out family roles. A good example of this occurred when we visited Joanne's house. She wanted her father to join the pretending. Joanne was the mother, her father was the daddy, and Joanne's mother was the baby. As the daddy arrived home from work, the mother was "tearing" roast beef for supper and trying to get the baby to bed. "Where's my supper?" roared daddy. "I'm hungry." "I want a drink of water," wailed the baby. "Get it yourself," snapped Joanne. The tension in the scene continued to escalate until finally the daddy suggested that they lock the baby in her room and eat their supper. It was clear that all three of the family members had adopted nasty roles, but none of them seemed particularly angry. In fact, the daddy seemed to be having a particularly good time yelling about suppertime.

When children choose to play out the punitive side of a parent role, they may be angry at their parents for some specific reason. More often they just are enjoying the good feeling that comes from pretending to be a powerful, angry person.

Another prestigious role that many preschool children assume in imaginative play is the role of teacher. The identification process has begun, and the children are learning to accept their teachers, for better or for worse, by imitating them. Jennifer's parents reported a play episode that illustrates very neatly the transition from being a student to being a pretend teacher. During the first week of school Jennifer had awakened her parents every morning with the announcement that it was Saturday and she didn't have to go to school. But when Saturday finally arrived, Jennifer was so involved in the process of accepting school that she wanted to recreate the classroom at home.

> "Let's play school. Mommy, you be Miss Virginia, and Daddy, you be Miss Virginia. Tell me to get out my morning book. Now watch me play. Now I'll be Miss Virginia. What color is this block, Mommy?"

Jennifer started by asking her parents to be the teacher, but since she had to tell them what to do, she soon became the teacher herself. As the play continued, Jennifer's parents got their first real glimpse of the kinds of activities that took place in Jennifer's classroom. At the same time, Jennifer had the opportunity to replay these events in the security of her home environment.

Jennifer's classroom seemed to be a happy place. For Jennifer the teacher represented a new attachment figure, an adult to take the place of parents during part of the day. Often the pretend classroom that young children create takes on a darker and more frightening cast. The teacher becomes quite an ogre, browbeating the children with dull lessons and threatening them with severe punishment. Joanne played school in this way. A collection of assorted dolls and stuffed animals were lined up and given a lecture:

> "Okay, class. I'm Ms. Rogers. Listen to me. We're learning numbers. Clown, you're not listening. You need to be punished. You need to be good or I'll hit you (hits him). Now you got to go home and tomorrow you better listen."

The prominence of negative comments by a pretend teacher alerts us to the fact that school experience is aggravating a child's fear of separation. The new and important adult in the child's world is generating feelings of insecurity. At the same time we need to consider the **very real possibility that the child is exaggerating. The pretending may relfect what the child fears will happen at school, not what actually happens. Playing school allows children to explore one of their**

Practice teaching.

worst fears, that a teacher is not a protective figure but a harsh jailer.

Although children often distort the reality of school in their pretending, a school is by necessity a different environment than a home. Because a group of children must be supervised by a small number of adults, behavior that is allowed at home may be restricted. In an effort to maintain their authority, teachers also may resort to threats and punishment more often than they would as parents with their own children. Playing out the role of punitive teacher, even in exaggerated form, helps children come to grips with these differences in a school environment.

The kind of good feelings that children get from pretending to be a power figure can be summarized by looking at doctor play. Pretending to be a doctor certainly gives children a sense of power. From the point of view of a child, a doctor's power is awesome. The orders of a doctor are even more binding than those of a parent. Most young children have heard their parents say, "We'll have to see what the doctor says," or "You have to do this because the doctor said so."

Occasionally, a preschool child pretends to be an extremely gentle doctor. More often the pretend doctor is an arbitrary, and somewhat punitive, character. The patient is poked, told to swallow pills, and given a shot. In this situation, it seems that the children are not really angry about a particular incident but are releasing general feelings of anxiety about doctors. Because of these feelings it is fun to be on the giving, rather than the receiving, end of medical treatment. And despite the punitive aspects of the doctor's role, there are definite limits if the children are to retain good feelings. Even a pretend doctor with a powerful weapon like a toy hypodermic or a rubber knife must not hurt his patient. This process of defining the limits of a power figure can be seen in "doctor" Zach's promise to his mother.

> Got to operate on you, Mommy.
> Yech—this is bad.
> I won't hurt you.
> You're lucky I'm a good doctor.

There are many other power roles that preschool children act out in imaginative play. A child may be a policeman, a fireman, a paramedic, or a truck driver. Again, in these roles we find the same mixture of nurturing and punitive behaviors that are characteristic of parent, teacher, and doctor play. On the one hand, power figures are helpful and protective; on the other hand, they are arbitrary and despotic. In general, children identify most strongly with the positive traits of a power figure, but they also can release feelings of anxiety and anger by adopting an authoritarian role.

MASTERING FEELINGS OF FEAR

Children feel good when they participate in jokes, reenact pleasant experiences, or place themselves in a position of power and prestige. They also feel good, or at least better, when they use imaginative play to overcome bad feelings. One of the major concerns that emerges in the imaginative play of preschool children is a fear of separation.

A part of growing up is spending more and more time away from home, and young children do demonstrate a strong desire to be independent. At the same time they are sensitive to the threat of separation. They become aware of separation in new forms. They realize that parents leave on a regular schedule for work, meetings, and other activities outside the home. A new and disturbing insight is that parents may take a trip away from home as part of their work. When Laura's father took a business trip to California, Laura knew that it was going to be a different kind of separation. After seeing him off on the airplane, she insisted on playing airport with her mother:

> *Laura:* Mommy, you go to the airport with me.
>
> *Mother:* Okay, I'll come. Do I need a ticket?
>
> *Laura:* I have a ticket for you. I'm going to need my purse.
>
> *Mother:* Are we on the airplane now?

Laura: Let's get our seat belts on. Mommy, the plane goes all by itself?

Mother: The pilot drives the plane.

Laura: I'll have to put a hat on. We're going to California to see Daddy. We're going to miss Daddy.

Divorce represents an extreme form of separation. Although children may appear to accept a divorce in a matter-of-fact way, the loss of a protector figure is a traumatic experience that arouses both sorrow and fear. Bad feelings that are camouflaged much of the time are quite likely to surface in imaginative play.

Chris's parents had been through a recent divorce. On the day of the final decree Chris was sent to his grandmother's home to help with the transition. She read him a good-night story, and brought him his favorite teddy bear, which served as his sleep companion. "I don't want my teddy bear," Chris told his grandmother as he threw it out of the bed. "I am a big boy now." In the following weeks Chris not only rejected the imaginary companions that had supported him, but his imaginative play declined to almost nothing. The loss of security in his relationships with real people had spilled over into his imaginary world.

Chris's feelings of being alone and afraid continued to grow. He did not like school and was convinced that rattlesnakes and ghosts lived along the road to school. He was frightened of a pony ride. Halloween terrified him. At the same time, though, he gradually began to rebuild his sense of security through imaginative play. He found a new imaginary companion in a bird that was bought as a birthday present shortly after the divorce. Chris uncovered the bird first thing each morning, gave him birdseed, and told him long stories about his plans for the day. The bird talked to Chris too. The two of them became so close that they were like brothers. As Chris told his mother one day, "Before I was a baby, I was a bird."

Chris also began to play out authority roles such as doctor or a policeman. Eventually he settled on the role of priest. In time he even pretended to be God. One day Chris pointed out the significance of this new imaginary role. If God could create a new friend for Chris in the form of a bird, he could fill the empty place in Chris's family as well. "I'm God," Chris announced to his mother, "and I'm going to make you a new man for Christmas." His costume for being God was the cover of the birdcage, which was thrown over his shoulder like a cape. Chris's bird had become his link with a world of security and hope. Draped in the birdcage cover he could set his world back in order.

In contrast to Chris, Zach's parents had been divorced for some time, and Zach seemed to have adjusted to this separation. As the youngest of three children in a close-knit family, he was surrounded with love and attention. But Zach's mother noticed that being lost was a recurrent theme in his pretending. One day Zach dressed up in some old hats and mittens. First he was a Chinese boy, then a baby boy, and then a little girl. Each character asked Zach's mother where Zach was. They wanted to play with Zach but he was lost. Finally Zach dressed as himself and was found.

When the family dog, Happy, wandered away from home and was really lost, Zach reconciled himself to the separation by pretending to call the dog on the phone:

> "Hello, Happy. Did you get lost in the jungle and you tried to find your way home to Zach? Zach misses you and you miss Zach. But you're okay, Happy. Bambi is in the jungle and you have lots of friends."

Zach recognized that his father was "lost" most of the time. They visited together on Sundays, but even this arrangement was tenuous. Pretending to call his father on the phone, he replayed the disappointment of having a visit canceled:

> "I miss you. Come play on Sunday. Why, you have bad news for me? Oh, you have bad news?"

Zach showed extra concern over not losing his mother. Kisses were especially important signs that all was well between them. Coming home from a visit with his father, Zach came up with an elaborate rationalization to explain why his mother had not received a good-bye kiss:

> "Mommy, before I left I forgot to give you a hug and a kiss, so I blew it to you. The hug and the kiss went to Mohio where they ran out of gas and couldn't find their way back to you."

The story of Jack and the Beanstalk was transformed by Zach into a story of separation. In his version there was no giant or golden hen, only a boy who couldn't find his mother:

> "A big weed was growing in front of Zach's house, and it goes climbing up to the sky. Mommy and Zach are on different leaves and they go running and running to find each other, and then they found each other, and Zach and Mommy gave each other a kiss."

Undoubtedly children respond in different ways to divorce. We cannot generalize on the basis of two families, but the experiences of Chris and Zach suggest that divorce heightens the separation fears of young children. They may reject toys they have been attached to, especially if these security objects are associated with the missing parent. Their sense of loss impels them to develop new attachments and to depend more heavily upon the parent who remains in the home. Imaginative play provides a medium for expressing and resolving this heightened fear. New attachments can be built through imaginary friendships, extra dependence on a parent or other attachment figure can be played out and losses can be rationalized.

Another frightening form of separation that preschool children have to deal with is the prospect of death. Although the children do not fully realize that death is permanent and irreversible, they are sufficiently concerned to deny the reality of death. This denial process may be very explicit. Connie, for example, was playing with a button box which belonged to her grandmother:

Connie: Where is Granny?

Mother: Your Granny is dead.

Connie: How did she die?

Mother: A heart attack—

Connie: What happened to her?

Mother: They buried her in the ground.

At this point Connie stretched out on the floor, closed her eyes, and placed her arms by her sides. Then she rubbed her eyes and asked, "Did she get dirt in her eyes?" When her mother tried to explain that dead people are placed in a coffin and they don't have any feelings, Connie got back down on the floor and resumed the same posture. "I'll just kick the dirt off," she explained and began to kick the floor.

Kori's denial of death took the form of a story which was prompted by the Old Gray Goose song that she had heard at school. "How does the old goose get dead?" Kori asked her mother after school. Kori's mother explained that the goose was very old and sick. A little later Kori recited her own version of the Old Gray Goose:

"Alesa's friend had a gray goose. They have a mill pond, and they feed her macaroni that isn't cooked yet 'cause that's what she likes, and it's never going to die, and I don't know why, and she's not going to stand on her head."

A second major concern appearing in imaginative play is a fear of danger. Increasingly aware of their physical vulnerability, preschool children imagine a host of threatening creatures around them. Wild animals lurk in dark corners, monsters and ghosts peer in through windows, and man-eating bugs crawl underfoot. One strategy for overcoming these dangers is to create an imaginary protector. John described a dragon that inhabited the living room lamp, but then went on to explain that his Superman doll attacked the dragon and everybody was safe. This approach also appeared in a story John told about the three little pigs:

> "The big bad wolf is coming to blow down the house, but the fireman is in bed sleeping, and he's gonna wake up and come to the house, and the pigs are gonna be saved."

Still another way children overcome a fear of animals is by turning them into pets. In the first chapter we described how Jad reassured his imaginary friend "Ja-Ja" that the wolves in the forest would not hurt them. Later at home he announced that a wolf named Sharon was living in the closet. Holding an invisible leash in his hand, Jad walked around the house with Sharon at his side. Christine hit upon the same solution in overcoming her fear of cockroaches. One day she met a cockroach in the middle of the kitchen floor. Instead of her usual terrified scream, Christine announced in a rather calm voice, "Look, Mother, Shirley is walking across the kitchen floor." Apparently Christine decided that if a bug was called by an ordinary name, it could not be very dangerous.

Another kind of physical danger that figures prominently in imaginative play is the possibility of a car accident. For days after a minor accident Brian crashed his toy cars into each other and drove an ambulance to the scene. "Accident here—stand back everybody," was the only dialogue that accompanied the play. Like a convalescent describing an operation, Brian used this recapitulation to dispel feelings of tension. Eventually, the box of toy cars was put aside and the crash incident forgotten.

Even when no real experience is involved, young children are preoccupied with the possibility of car accidents. As they play with toy cars it is almost certain that there will be an intentional "accident," and often the results are serious enough to rush the victim to an imaginary hospital. Matt told us about a pretend accident that was especially vivid. His story illustrates the kind of fear children are able to express when they pretend with toy cars:

"I had a dream that I was in a car, and we bashed into someone, and blood was dripping down. Paul was there too. We had bandages down our knees. Mother was in the back seat. I was driving the car. I drived too fast and I bashed ourselves. We bashed into a man. He had to go to the hospital to check his heartbeat and check his blood pressure and get bandages."

There are many other physical dangers that appear in imaginative play—thunder, lightning, fire, poison, robbery, and water in various forms. Like wild animals and accidents, these physical dangers are controlled through imaginative strategies. Amy, who was scared of her swimming pool, put on her mother's bathing suit and went swimming in her mother's bed. Kori handled her fear of hair washing by repeatedly scrubbing her doll's hair. Angela reenacted a frightening car wash experience with a big brush, soap and water, and a hair dryer.

Although a danger may be real enough, the fears of preschool children often are imaginary. It is what they imagine that frightens them, not what actually exists. Wolves are indeed dangerous, but there were no wolves in the neighborhoods where the children lived. Deep water could be fatal, but the children could not drown in a shower or car wash. It is because their fears are based primarily on imagination that imaginary solutions make so much sense.

Storms fit into the category of dangers that are often feared for the wrong reason. Jennifer heard her family discuss preparations for a hurricane and recognized the feeling of danger. Using her imagination and bits of conversation, she gave form to the shadowy menace:

Jennifer: I don't want that hurricane to come.

Nana: Do you know what a hurricane is?

Jennifer: It's a one-eyed thing that travels and doesn't know which way it's going.

Later, in the grocery store, Jennifer overheard a woman say to the clerk, "I think I'll buy some cheese; cheese is good for hurricanes." Jennifer's face brightened. "Nana," she suggested, "why don't we buy some cheese to feed to the hurricane?"

Like Jennifer, Jad recognized that storms are dangerous things that must be dealt with. He had even devised an imaginary solution right in his own backyard. When we went to his house, Jad showed us a rotating lawn sprinkler. "I work on it when a storm comes," he said in a serious tone. "Water comes out of these holes and kills the storm." We agreed that the rain from the previous day had stopped. "It is very dangerous," Jad continued. "It could kill you." But he added quickly, "I won't let it kill nobody." And he showed us how to turn off the storm-killing machine by pressing a certain spot on the sprinkler. Apparently Jad had associated the falling rain with the water from the sprinkler and then imagined that the sprinkler, which could be turned on and off, could be used to control the rain. The rainstorm, an imaginary creature, could be killed by another imaginary creature that spouted water in a similar way.

COPING WITH ANGER AND JEALOUSY

Imaginative play also helps children deal with feelings of anger, frustration, and jealousy. When a new sibling is born, it is natural for preschool children to feel anger toward the baby. The birth disrupts the established pattern within the family, and the baby becomes the center of attention. The first reaction is often a direct attack, which may be disguised as imaginative play.

When Jennifer's baby brother came home from the hospital, she tried to hide her feelings. "I am patting Kenneth to sleep," Jennifer announced as she patted him gently on the rear. "I am the best patter in the world," she continued as the patting got more and more vigorous. The next day she approached her brother with a fly swatter in her hand. "What are you doing?" her mother said as she caught the fly swatter in midair. "I am pretending there's a fly on Kenneth," Jennifer replied innocently.

We have already described how Kori reacted to the news of her mother's pregnancy by growing ten babies in her tummy. When her brother was born, so were her own ten babies, but the babies were sent away to live in another house, "near the drug store on Huron Street." The real Brennan could not be dismissed as easily as ten imaginary babies. One day Kori approached the problem by drawing a scribble on a piece of paper:

"This is a picture of a crab for my baby brother, Brennan. The crab has teeth. It can bite. It bites little babies. It doesn't bite hard."

That night as she put Kori to bed, Kori's mother helped Kori express in words her angry feelings toward her brother. Talking about these feelings helped some. The next day Kori drew another scribble. "I made a baby crab," Kori told her mother. "It has no teeth. It won't bite my baby brother Brennan."

A second reaction is to participate with the baby whenever the baby is getting special attention. Jennifer's mother found that if she nursed Kenneth on the bed, that was the very place Jennifer needed to put her stuffed animals to sleep. If her mother was sitting with Kenneth on the rocker, it was the only chair in the whole house that Jennifer could use as a car.

Like Jennifer, Jamie was disturbed by the fact that his baby brother, Benjamin, was being breast-fed. "Can I drink milk out of your nipples?" he asked his mother. Without giving his mother a chance, Jamie answered his own question. "No, you can't. You have teeth." A little later he asked his mother if he could play with her nursing pads. Jamie was delighted when she gave him a handful of pads and immediately used them as all-purpose props. The pads were used as toilet paper, napkins, and handkerchiefs. They became blankets to cover up his miniature doll characters and Band-Aids when he played doctor. Frustrated in his efforts to join the baby, Jamie assuaged his feelings of being left out by using the nursing pads in imaginative play.

The feelings aroused by a new sibling are frequently reflected in doll play. In fact many parents give a preschool child a new doll when a baby is born. The doll serves as a substitute when a child cannot handle a baby, and feelings of anger and jealousy can be directed at the doll without any harm being done to the baby. Jennifer's initial respose to her new doll was violent. "I don't want that baby doll," she exploded, but in time she adopted the baby and her mother found it was easier to nurse Kenneth. Instead of crawling into her mother's lap, Jennifer sat on her own rocker and nursed her doll by lifting up one side of her shirt. Jamie too used a doll as a substitute for his own participation. "You don't have teeth, Teddy," he explained to his bear, "so you have to have milk from mommy." And he pressed the teddy bear against his mother's breast.

Kori's doll play was more elaborate. She and her mother had evolved a style of play in which her mother spoke for the doll. In that way the doll could express complicated feelings. The signal for initiating this kind of doll play was for Kori to say, "Ask Raggie why she's crying." When her mother asked the question, Kori would answer, "You say—" This was the signal for Kori's mother to take the part of Raggie. If Kori's mother guessed the wrong reason for Raggie's crying, Kori would correct her.

Shortly before Kori's brother was born, a close family friend gave birth and Kori accompanied her parents on a visit to the new baby. Kori watched very closely as the mother breast-fed the new baby. Predictably, that night Kori initiated the back and forth dialogue with Raggie. "Ask Raggie why she's crying." Kori's mother had no trouble figuring out what Raggie was supposed to say.

Raggie: (Kori's mother speaking) I want my nursing.

   Kori: You can't nurse now. The babies (the ten imaginary babies in her tummy) are nursing.

Raggie: Oh.

   Kori: But you can sit on my shoulders if you want.

A few days later, when Kori initiated the crying routine, her mother changed the script.

   Kori: Ask Raggie why she's crying.

Mother: Why are you crying, Raggie?

   Kori: You say.

Raggie: (Kori's mother speaking) I'm jealous.

   Kori: Why are you jealous?

Raggie: I don't want you to hold the babies and their sisters (the imaginary babies in Kori's tummy). I want you to hold me.

   Kori: I'll hold you in a little while.

Raggie: I want you to love me.

   Kori: I always love you, Raggie. Now the babies got off my hand. You can sit here on my hand.

Feelings of jealousy toward siblings can also be expressed in imaginative play with other children. Scott and Brandon are brothers who spend a good deal of time in each other's company. They have discovered that when each of them adopts a power role, they can express feelings of sibling rivalry in a way that is acceptable to their mother. Their power confrontations are usually modeled after television shows. One brother is the sheriff while the other is the bank robber. Or one brother represents the cowboys while the other represents the attacking Indians. In the last chapter we described the zest with which the brothers reenacted a *Star Wars* battle. Neither brother wins every time. Apparently Brandon, the older brother, recognizes that he had better let Scott win once in a while if he wants Scott to keep playing.

Marcus, a four-year-old with two-year-old twin brothers, was contending with more powerful negative feelings. He gave the appearance of being a mild and nonaggressive youngster. But behind his gentle and innocent look Marcus seemed to be struggling with enormous feelings of jealousy and anger. Violent actions and ideas constantly appeared in his imaginative play. Marcus told the following story while playing with two five-year-old friends:

"A monster came and hurt me behind the knee and there was a scratch there. And I went home and got a bat and whacked the monster. Then the monster threw a giant rock at me, and I threw it back, and I got a knife and cut off his head."

"Did you bury the monster?" his friend asked.

"No, I cut him into little pieces and put him in a pan and cooked him for dinner."

Stacy, like Marcus, had difficulty sharing her parents with a very assertive sibling. At school she often chose to play in the housekeeping area with another girl named Gina. Gina became the bossy mother, while Stacy was a sullen daughter. With a scowl on her face Stacy confronted her mother one minute and then the next minute begged for her attention. She would yell at Gina that she did not want any food, and then after receiving it anyway, pretend to eat by putting her face in the plate and gobbling loudly. The only attention Stacy succeeded in getting from her pretend mother came in the form of spankings and verbal abuse, which only made her more contrary.

The teacher informed us that Stacy had an older brother, who seemed to be favored by the parents. Certainly Stacy's imaginative play indicated that she felt rejected by her parents. One day Stacy tried out an imaginary solution to this problem. She became the son in the family instead of the daughter. In order to call attention to this radical transformation, she pretended to undress. Standing behind several chairs to simulate the privacy of a bedroom, Stacy announced to the rest of the family that she was naked. Then she pretended to take a shower and to urinate by holding an imaginary penis. Stacy seemed pleased with this sex change, although Gina punished her exhibitionism by banging a plate over her head.

Children like Stacy and Marcus are struggling with such strong negative emotions that it is disturbing at times to watch their pretending. Some difficult questions come to mind.

Can pretending contribute to bad feelings as well as alleviating them: Can a fearful child sometimes become more fearful as a result of pretending; Can an angry child become more angry? In addition, can pretending be an escape from reality as well as a way of coping with reality?

We are not sure of the answers to these questions. It is obvious that imaginative play is not a panacea for bad feelings. Powerful feelings of anger and jealousy cannot be eliminated through play. At the same time, we are confident that in most cases pretending does help children cope with bad feelings. It releases tension and gives the children a sense of control. It takes the edge off of negative emotions.

Looking over the examples presented we see a continuum. At one end are situations in which bad feelings are relatively mild, and the children are clearly aware that they are pretending. At the other end of the continuum are situations in which bad feelings seem to overwhelm the child, and the distinction between fantasy and reality is blurred. Scott and Brandon know they are only pretending to kill each other, and it seems that this pretense helps them get along with each other. On the other hand, there is an intensity in Marcus's account of killing the monster that makes us wonder if he really believes it.

It seems to us that bad feelings which are very strong may be heightened when first expressed in imaginative play. Precisely because the children do not recognize their play as imaginary, the play itself can increase feelings of fear or anger. However, this phenomenon is only temporary. More experience with an imaginary idea leads a child to realize that it is just pretend. An imaginary theme involving bad feelings is not static. It changes, and the direction of change is toward the end of the continuum where bad feelings are controlled and pretending is clearly recognized.

We can take Jad's storm-killing machine as an example of this process. Jad was not overwhelmed by a fear of storms, but the earnestness with which he explained the machine indicated considerable concern. Jad seemed to believe the machine really worked—but not in any ordinary sense. It worked by special magic. Already there was a break between reality and the way this machine worked. We would predict that if Jad continues to use the lawn sprinkler in this way, he will become increasingly aware that he is pretending. The sense of control that he presently gets from the storm-killing machine will rest on a more secure foundation, and he will be able to cope even better with the imaginary dangers of a storm.

GAINING REAL POWER

Despotic or benevolent, punitive or nurturing, children enjoy the illusion of power when they pretend. But imaginative play also provides opportunities to express real power over other people, and this real power produces good feelings. Children can place themselves in command and have adults do their bidding.

Kori had invited her Nana to come over to her pretend nursery school. "You sit here," she commanded, "and you play with the little blocks. No, not the block with the cow picture. That one belongs to Raggie." Kori's pregnant aunt, who had been watching the scene, asked if she could come to school too. "This school is only for Nanas and mommies and children," responded Kori. "But I'm a mommy," countered her aunt. "Can't I please come to your school?" "No," said Kori emphatically. "It's only for mothers who are not fat."

Usually children select the best roles for themselves and assign less desirable parts to adults. A parent is asked to play the baby role when children want to play Mommy and Daddy. Children are the doctors while adults are their helpless patients. Adults must be the customers so that the children can play the more exciting role of waiter. As Chad put it when playing train with his mother, "I'll be the conductor and you be the caboose."

Just as adults usually let children set the roles in imaginative play, they allow children to contradict their suggestions about how the plot should unfold. More than once we saw instances in which the children highly valued the participation of their parents but made a special point of contradicting their parents' ideas.

Children gain a sense of power by directing the imaginative play of adults. They also can use imaginative play to argue with parents. "Kori, would you mind picking up your toys?" Nana requested. "I can't, Nana," Kori explained in a polite tone. "I have to go take care of Acky and all the little sisters." Acky and her sisters, Kori's imaginary babies, were ready-made excuses whenever there was something Kori did not want to do. Of course, the pretense worked beautifully. A three-year-old who says, "No, I won't!" is considered defiant, but it is hard to get angry with a little girl who has to take care of her babies.

Several other children discovered that pretending could provide a quick rationalization for avoiding parental directives. Zachary did not want to wear the pair of pajamas his mother had selected. "But I can't wear pajamas to bed," he explained to his mother. "The mouse and the kitty (on the pajamas) run all over and tickle me all night long." Jennifer did some quick thinking to get herself out of trouble. "Why did you crayon on the wall?" Jennifer's mother queried with obvious annoyance. "But Mommy," Jennifer explained. "I just drew a picture of you."

Pretending is useful not only for getting out of work or keeping out of trouble, it can also be a tool for manipulating adult behavior. Jennifer wanted to play with her stroller, which unfortunately was located in the family room in front of the television set. A scary monster had just appeared on the screen, and although Jennifer would never admit to being frightened, she was not about to risk a close encounter. "Mommy," she asked in a casual tone, "would you please get my stroller? It's a little bit stuck in the mud."

Jennifer's ruse greatly amused her mother, and she was happy to oblige Jennifer. Sometimes the child's attempt to manipulate is more strident. While riding in the car Brian's mother and father were talking to each other. Brian tried to get his mother's attention by tapping her on the shoulder. She turned around and said, "Daddy and I are talking right now." Brian retorted indignantly, "You can't say that to me—I'm in the control tower."

Although Brian's answer surprised his parents and he succeeded in getting his parents' attention, there are limits to the effectiveness of imaginative play as a manipulative ploy. Jill and her mother were at odds over whether or not she should have a cookie before dinner. "Absolutely not," her mother insisted, "and there's no use arguing." Jill turned toward her brother Ken. "Let's play house. You're the mother and I'm the little girl." Then she asked her new mother, "Mommy, may I have a cookie?" Probably Jill realized that Ken would not get her the cookie, but perhaps she hoped to wear down her mother's resistance with this imaginative idea. Despite the ingenuity of her scheme, Jill did not get a cookie until after dinner.

We usually think of manipulation in negative terms, but these efforts at manipulation do not strike us as being very negative. Most children discover that whining and temper tantrums are not effective ways of gaining control over adults. Imaginative play, however, is a viable alternative. Adults are free to deny the fantasies of children if they feel they must. If they go along with the pretending, attempts to manipulate can lead to a compromise in which both adults and children are satisfied.

For example, Amy tended to ignore instructions about getting ready for bed unless her father assumed the role of Chicken Daddy, which meant that Amy asked him questions and he answered in "chicken." As long as he continued clucking, Amy's father was allowed to give Amy a bath, wash her hair, and tuck her into bed. Having daddy turn into a chicken was an effective way for Amy to manipulate her father into giving her special attention. At the same time, it eliminated hassles over bedtime chores, which pleased Amy's parents.

Brett used a similar approach when he wanted some extra attention from his mother. "Ding-dong," he would say, making the sound of a doorbell:

> "Hi, Mrs. Harris. My name is Wiggy the dog. My mommy said I could play with Brett."

Brett's mother continued the conversation for a few moments, asking Wiggy what color he was, where he lived, etc. If Brett started to get carried away with his role, perhaps trying to eat food off the floor like a dog, his mother simply asked him to go find Brett. In this way, he could leave the room, change roles gracefully, and come back as himself.

Brett's mother found that the dog identity helped overcome Brett's resistance to naps. Brett felt he was too old to take a nap; his mother disagreed. One day Brett came up with the idea of pretending to be a dog and sleeping under the bed. This was a fine compromise. Brett's mother accomplished her goal, and Brett was able to adopt a role that brought him special attention within the family.

The real power that children can exercise through imaginative play certainly produces good feelings. Yet it is the promise of transcending the everyday limitations of childhood that gives the imaginative play its special appeal. Good feelings are wishes fulfilled, and in the world of make-believe adult rules and regulations are suspended. We can sum up the message of this chapter with the following example from Terry's imaginative play. Placing a miniature doll in a toy car, Terry announced that the doll was named Terry and that he was driving the car all by himself:

Mother: Is he old enough to drive a car?

Terry: He's four already.

Mother: You have to be sixteen to drive a car.

Terry: He doesn't know that. He'll be careful.

Children, like Terry, who can take the wheel in imaginative play, have found a powerful way to feel good about themselves. With the magic of pretending at their command, they have greater freedom to express

Terry driving a car without a license.

their feelings, and the restrictions imposed by the real world can be faced more cheerfully.

FROM THE LITERATURE

A study by Wendy Matthews (1977) illustrates how preschool children seek to be powerful when they play out parent roles.° She videotaped the free play of four pairs of boys and four pairs of girls over a three-day period. Each pair was observed for one hour a day while playing in a room filled with toys. The children were between 4.0 and 4.4 years of age and had not known each other before the study began.

Both boys and girls spent approximately 30 percent of their imaginative play in meal preparation. Usually cooking was seen as the prerogative of the mother, but the father role was associated with certain treats, such as bringing home and serving ice cream. The boys chose to spend little of their time on other household tasks, although a boy playing the father role would occasionally help the mother. For example, one pretend father fixed a "broken" ironing board, while another plugged in the iron for his wife. Fathers were prominent as drivers—driving to work, driving a burning boat, telling the mother which car to take, etc.

In contrast to the boys, the girls spent 45 percent of their play time in household tasks other than meal preparation. In fact the girl pairs preferred the mother role so strongly that frequently they both played female roles:

> *Karen:* I'll be the mother, and you can be the grandmother, okay?
> *Kathy:* Okay.
> *Karen:* And who can be the father?
> *Kathy:* No one. . . . You don't need a father.

The mother's role was perceived by the girls as being powerful. Mothers knew where everything in the house belonged. Mothers also had a special responsibility for taking care of sickness. In various episodes mother figures told the father that the baby was sick, took the baby to the hospital, introduced the family to the doctor, and discussed an illness with the doctor on the telephone. The mother role was so

°Wendy Schempp Matthews, "Sex Role Perception, Portrayal, and Preference in the Fantasy Play of Young Children" (Paper presented at the Biennial Meeting of the Society for Research in Child Development, New Orleans, La., March 17–20, 1977).

closely associated with the doctor that one pretend mother even delivered babies.

Particularly interesting is the author's conclusion that the boys and girls in her study seemed equally nurturing toward babies, with boys being more nurturant in a father role and girls in a mother role.

PART TWO

THE ROLE
OF THE ADULT
IN ENCOURAGING
IMAGINATIVE PLAY

Chapter Four

The Adult as Observer
What parents and teachers can learn
by watching children pretend

A primary objective of *Just Pretending* is to describe ways in which parents and teachers can encourage the imaginative play of young children. In the first three chapters, we have provided the rationale for encouraging imaginative play by describing the benefits of pretending. In the final chapters we focus on the role of the adult in encouraging imaginative play.

The most basic role of an adult in imaginative play is to be an observer. Observation shows us the themes that interest a child and guides our attempts to join in the pretending. The sharper our observation, the easier it is to respond to the imaginative ideas of a child. By definition, good observation means paying close attention to significant behavior and events. This means that we must make some assumptions about what behaviors are significant. Assumptions are based in part on what kind of pretending we expect, or what we consider typical at a particular age. By familiarizing ourselves with play characteristics that are typical of different age groups, we can place a child's pretending in a larger context. Our assumptions will be more valid, and our anticipation of new developments more precise. In the first part of this chapter we describe some typical characteristics of imaginative play among two-, three-, four-, and five-year-old children and also identify some play characteristics that tend to be sex-related.

In the second part of this chapter, we discuss a way to observe the play styles of preschool children. We find it useful to categorize these play styles as being actor-type or producer-type. Within these broad categories there are several variations. Children who pretend as actors may assume a direct role in a scene, like an actor in a play. They may dance, put on a talent show, or turn themselves into mechanical objects. Children pretending in the style of a producer-director take more of a backstage position. They control the pretend event from a detached perspective. One child may create a pretend story in the manner of a scriptwriter. Another child may prefer to be a set designer by drawing an imaginary scene or by constructing an imaginary environment. A third child may become a director, animating a pretend world of miniature toys.

A knowledge of normal play patterns and a framework for categorizing play styles make our observation more productive. Equally important is an ability to identify the characteristics of a play environment that may be influencing the nature of the play. In the third section of this chapter we identify specific features of preschool settings that influence the quality and quantity of pretending. At the same time we make suggestions about how and what to look for in the classroom environment.

When we talk about play patterns, play styles, and play settings we are making broad generalizations about children. These generalizations may be useful as guidelines, but they don't tell us very much about an individual child. Our real interest must always be in recognizing the unique aspects of each child's pretending and in identifying each child's distinctive patterns. In a manner of speaking, we can think of each child's imagination as a kaleidoscope that reflects in bits and pieces a child's impressions of life. As we put these pieces together and identify larger patterns we have a special opportunity to share a child's view of the world.

TYPICAL ASPECTS OF IMAGINATIVE PLAY: TWO YEARS OLD

REPETITION OF FAMILIAR ROUTINES—Two-year-olds at play, whether they are driving their trucks in a sandbox, feeding their dolls, or preparing dinner for the family, are hard at work replaying fragments of everyday experience. These bits and pieces of familiar routine are repeated over and over again, with little effort to integrate them into a longer sequence. When Heather served a tea party to her friends, the entire routine consisted of pouring tea, burping the baby, and pouring the tea again. Jamie's teddy bear play consisted of putting the bear in the cradle, saying, "Night-night, teddy," lifting him out of the cradle, and starting all over again.

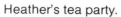
Heather's tea party.

INFLEXIBILITY—There is an inflexibility in the constant repetition. Andrew, a two-year-old who was riding his tricycle around the dining room table, stopped every time he passed the closet where the vacuum cleaner was kept. Getting off his trike, Andrew tapped the front wheel with the wand of the vacuum, made a kind of "pssss" sound, and continued on his way. We suggested that he check the back tires too, but Andrew paid no attention.

ACTION-BASED PRETENDING—While Andrew's tricycle play is a good example of the rigidity of two-year-old pretending, it also demonstrates another typical characteristic. The pretending of the two-year-old is action-based. Although the youngster may use words or sound effects to go along with the actions, the words are not very important. The essence of the pretending is in the sequence of actions that the child performs.

NO NEED FOR LANGUAGE—Jennifer, also two-years-old, was playing with a dollhouse. Once she had it set up to her satisfaction, she meticulously lined up each miniature doll character and turned its head around so that it was facing the window. For every two characters that she managed to stand up, a third character toppled over, but Jennifer persisted with the task. Finally, her father was overcome with curiosity and asked her what she was doing. "Standing up the people," Jennifer explained, "so they can watch the sun." Although Jennifer was able to explain her behavior, language was not an important part of the pretending. She felt no need to direct the doll characters nor to provide a running commentary of the imaginary scene.

IMPULSIVITY—Another interesting characteristic of a two-year-old pretending is the way that props are used. On the one hand, play is very much influenced by props. From the two-year-old point of view, keys are for turning, hammers are for banging, and tea sets are for serving food. But while the discovery of a realistic prop may prompt the child to pretend, a pretend theme can be played out just as easily without any kind of prop. Jamie turned on his "wheeling car" with an invisible key, and Jennifer poured invisible clam chowder into a phantom cup.

This apparent contradiction between the effect of realistic props and the prop-free nature of much of the pretending seems to be due to the impulsivity of two-year-old play. The very second a two-year-old finds a toy or comes up with an idea, the pretend play must begin. Often the toy prompts the idea for pretending. If the idea comes first, though, a child will seize on any handy object as a prop or carry out the play with no object at all.

SERIOUS BUSINESS—A final characteristic of two-year-old play is its generally serious tone. Erik came hobbling into the room wearing his mother's shoes, cradling a coconut in his arms, and humming "Rock-a-bye-baby" to himself. When everyone started laughing, Erik was highly indignant.

As we can see from our examples, pretending at this age has several characteristics that give it a special flavor. Two-year-olds characteristically play out themes that are familiar to them: eating, sleeping, shopping, taking care of a baby, or driving a car. The replay is short, repetitive, and episodic. Once a pretend routine is established, it can become rigid and ritualistic, and the adult must not interfere until the ritual is completed. Language may accompany the play, but it is not used just to set the stage or lengthen the plot. Props are used when they are available, but it is just as satisfactory for the two-year-old to use unusual substitutes or invisible props. Finally, pretending tends to be serious business, and a parent who shows amusement provokes a burst of temper.

THREE YEARS OLD

Although a three-year-old birthday does not bring out a sudden shift in play behavior, there is a recognizable difference between the pretending of a two-year-old and that of a three-year-old. Let's look at Mandy, age three, as she goes on a picnic with her mother.

Mandy: I'll be the mommy and you be the little girl. We go on a picnic. Now you sit down.

Mother: Is this where we're having the picnic?

Mandy: Yes, watch out for bugs. You want some milk?

Mother: Oh, I'd love some. This milk is delicious.

Mandy: You want some carrot?

Mother: (Touching large end to her lips) Best carrot I've ever tasted.

Mandy: No, silly. Don't eat that end. That end doesn't taste good.

Mother: Oh, you're right. What else are we going to eat?

Mandy: You see any bugs? Don't let the bugs bite you.

Mother: I'd like some dessert.

> *Mandy:* I got some birthday cake. I cut you some?
>
> *Mother:* Sounds good, but how about a cup of coffee?
>
> *Mandy:* Soon you get coffee—I'm colding it. Let's sing Happy Birthday.

PREPLANNING—Several differences between two- and three-year-old play are evident in this example. An obvious development is the element of preplanning. Mandy did not just see a picnic basket and launch into play. First she filled the basket with props in order to carry out her idea. A second obvious development is the assignment of roles. Typical of three-year-olds, Mandy reverses the usual roles. She becomes the mother and her mother becomes the little girl. Mandy is the authority figure, serving the food, warning of bugs, and even telling her mother the right way to eat a carrot.

SUSTAINED BY LANGUAGE—Mandy's imaginary picnic is very much created and sustained by language. She is old enough to carry on a lengthy dialogue with her mother, and her statement "I'm colding it" (the coffee) illustrates the fresh, creative use of language that is characteristic of many three-year-olds. The conversation between Mandy and her mother is the means by which the picnic scene is stretched out and a variety of details are added. The dialogue discourages ritualistic repetition while it encourages an orderly unfolding of the plot. Words are available to make the original plan explicit ("We go on a picnic") and to structure each successive step in the episode.

The themes in play at this age still tend to revolve around family activities, although more attention is paid to special events like a picnic. A hint of danger may appear, as in Mandy's concern over bugs, but the danger, like the excitement, is muted and rather prosaic.

CLEARLY MARKED SEQUENCES—The sequence is clearly marked in most three-year-old pretending. Yet an episode may slide from one event to another or the child may switch from one role to another without warning. In the picnic scene, where Mandy's mother takes a passive role, we see the theme drift imperceptibly from picnic to birthday party.

RIGID USE OF PROPS—The importance given to props and the inability to proceed with the play until the right prop is found gives a new kind of rigidity to three-year-old play. The picnic basket and plastic food are an integral part of every pretend picnic that Mandy initiates. Whereas the rigidity of earlier play stems from a ritualistic repetition of an action sequence, the rigidity of the three-year-old is often tied to the insistence on particular props.

BEGINNING OF PEER PLAY—The pretending skill of children at this age is great enough to allow them to join the imaginative play of a peer group. Even at three years old, however, a pretend episode with a peer is not apt to last long, especially if the peer is the same age. The children are not flexible in handling difference of opinion. In the following scene we see Mandy's inability to sustain play with another child, who is not as accommodating as her mother:

> *Derek:* Mandy, let's take the doll to the beauty shop and color her hair purple.
>
> *Mandy:* Purple?
>
> *Derek:* Purple is my favorite color.
>
> *Mandy:* My doll has soap in her eyes! (Mandy tries to wash the soap out but Derek pulls the doll away.)
>
> *Derek:* We're losing the purple, Mandy!
>
> *Mandy:* No—soap in her eyes!
>
> *Derek:* There is no soap in her eyes.
>
> *Mandy:* Yes—soap in dolly's eyes—soap in dolly's eyes.
>
> *Derek:* Okay, I'll wash it.
>
> *Mandy:* I'm making soup.

Derek, who is older, eventually gives in and follows Mandy's lead, but by this time her ideas have turned elsewhere. He starts to rinse the doll's hair, and she continues to mix her soup. The play lasts for another ten minutes, with no interaction between the two friends.

PROJECTING THE FEELINGS OF CHARACTERS—In the last example Mandy's doll was a passive participant. Often the dolls that three-year-olds play with have become more complex characters. The two-year-old typically directs, bosses, or manipulates a doll. Three-year-olds can be just as bossy, but we see more signs that a doll has been imbued with human characteristics. The doll has feelings and personality, and maybe even a voice. Let's look at Kori as she speaks for her dolls, expresses their feelings, and then plays the part of referee.

> *Kori:* (Speaking to the dolls Raggie and Alyse) Oh, you're fighting. Why are you fighting?

Kori: (As Raggie) I wanted this Count and I telled Alyse she could have the other Count.

Kori: (Holding up Alyse and shaking her vehemently) Now, you shouldn't do that Alyse. Don't you ever do that again.

Kori: (Putting down Alyse and picking up Raggie) Oh, you can have your Count now.

Kori: (Turning back to Alyse) Oh, Alyse, you don't want that Count anyway.

Kori not only projects her ideas about fairness onto the dolls, but also discovers a way of helping poor Alyse resign herself to giving up a toy. This particular episode is sophisticated for a three-year-old, but it is a good example of the three-year-old's emerging ability to recognize and project feelings.

Three-years-old is a transition period between the primitive pretending of the two-year-old and the more advanced pretending of four- and five-year-olds. In contrast with twos, three-year-olds have better developed themes and more attention is paid to sequence, detail, and continuity. Planning is beginning to occur as evidenced by the preselection of appropriate props. A very noticeable advance is the introduction of dialogue both to establish the pretense and to describe the actions and thoughts of the characters. Three-year-olds not only talk to pretend characters but will also talk for the pretend characters. Finally, we see the beginning of peer play and the sharing of play themes and ideas.

TYPICAL FOUR- AND FIVE-YEAR-OLD PLAY

As we watch fours and fives engage in pretend play, still further developmental strides are evident. The three-year-old is concerned with reenacting daily events. The four- and five-year-olds are exploring new ideas and trying out new experiences.

DANGER-PACKED THEMES—Typical four- and five-year-old play is noisy, urgent, and intense with an aura of excitement and danger. Both in the choice of theme and the way it is acted out we see a growing fascination with matters of life and death. *Star Wars* is reenacted, superheroes emerge from the television, villains are hunted down, and wild animals captured. The everyday themes of the twos and threes have been replaced by the exciting, danger-packed themes of the fours. Adult pretenders are replaced with peers, who have a special talent for keeping up the level of the excitement.

Scott: (Shouting through a megaphone) Fire! Fire! Get out. Everybody—it's on fire.

Brandon: (Throws himself on the floor and groans in an exaggerated way.) Help—help—ooooh—Awwww—ooooh!

Scott: Doctor Bracket (talking on a phone) some boys fell through the floor.

Brandon: (Turns over and increases the intensity of his groaning and moaning.)

Scott: Got to take your blood pressure. Bad blood pressure. Number 16—the heart's not beating.

Brandon: (Gives out one enormous groan and then stays still as Scott pretends to plug in some apparatus. Suddenly, he jumps to his feet.)

Scott: (On the phone again) Heart's beating—he's okay now.

While some children like Brandon and Scott express their concern with danger by taking the role of rescuer, other four- and five-year-olds show a stronger tendency to take the role of aggressor. During a home visit Todd disappeared rather suddenly from the living room and came back dressed in a black jacket and mask. "I'm Frankenstein," he warned in a low, ominous voice with his hand held up in a threatening gesture. Walking stiffly across the room, he knocked down a tower that he had built with his mother, kicked a couple of blocks and then threw a stuffed elephant at Pooh Bear. Following a suggestion from his mother to calm down, Todd gave a new twist to the Frankenstein role.

"Come on, Pooh Bear. We'll make a booby trap for the elephant. Now, elephant, you stay in the booby trap. You're trapped forever, Mr. Elephant—and you can't get out."

Again Todd's mother intervened and suggested that maybe Mr. Elephant could get himself out of the trap by scaring Frankenstein.

"Frankenstein is not scared of anything," Todd announced. "He's not scared of fire at all. He's not scared of water at all. He's not afraid of noise bombs. He breaks them. And he's not afraid of spiders and he's not afraid of kisses."

During the whole harangue Todd continued to grimace and growl.

SOCIAL LEARNING—The imaginative play of four and fives becomes even more wild and danger-filled when a group of youngsters get together. Mothers may throw up their hands in despair as their pre-schoolers screech through the house or dive off the beds playing monster, Batman, or Wonder Woman. This kind of wild, supercharged play, without plot or dialogue, may appear to be regressive. Actually, a lot of social learning takes place in this wild kind of pretending. Children are learning to cope with mild aggression, to establish and recognize dominance, and to focus on the actions and reactions of the other children in the group. Most important, they are gaining a sense of group solidarity and common purpose which lays the groundwork for later, more organized, play.

TRUE INVENTIVENESS—Although the salience of the peer group and the emergence of group pretending is perhaps the most striking difference between the play of the younger and older preschool child, there are also some critical differences that could be thought of as intellectual advances. The two-year-old is concerned with the replay of familiar events. The three-year-old also replays familiar events but with a greater repertoire of experiences from which to draw material. By four and five there is a true inventive element in much of the pretend play. Even in a situation where the child is replaying a real experience, we see a greater elaboration of detail and an infusion of new ideas. Props are gathered more selectively, costumes are more complete, and familiar incidents are given a new twist.

Wendy and her mother were going in a plane to New York. The airplane consisted of two kitchen chairs which were placed side by side in the family room:

> *Wendy:* My baby doll, Laurie, is coming with us. We need to bring a pillow for her.
>
> *Mother:* Is there anything else we need?
>
> *Wendy:* I have the suitcase and my purse. You carry the camera.
>
> *Mother:* (Sitting down in one of the chairs) Are we ready to take off?
>
> *Wendy:* We're ready. Do up your seat belt (pretends to do up her own). Now, I've got to give Laurie her medicine. Here, Laurie, take your medicine and be careful not to spill the water.

The airplane trip was quite an eventful affair. Wendy took her mother's

"Here, Laurie, take your medicine!"

picture, read a story to Laurie, ordered a soda, fed Laurie lunch, ate her own lunch, and finally combed her own hair in preparation for landing. As the plane landed, Wendy waved out the window to Aunt Lolly, gathered up her belongings, and said good-bye to the empty chairs.

In Wendy's replay of an airplane trip we see not only a fluency of ideas and an elaboration of detail but also a dramatic change in the amount and quality of the dialogue and exposition. Language is used more and more to set the scene, create the mood, and explain the pretense. Before Wendy begins to gather the props, she tells her mother that they are going to New York on a National Airlines jet. As we watch Wendy gather up the items that she needs for the airplane trip: suitcase, purse, doll, reading material, and notebook, we recognize that collecting the props is an integral part of the play. In order to go on a trip you need to do advance planning. This advance planning, which was just emerging in three-year-old play, is still not perfected at four. Wendy had to leave the plane after takeoff to get the medicine for her doll.

DISTINGUISHING REAL FROM PRETEND—Another intellectual development that we see emerging at four and five is the ability to make more explicit distinctions between real and pretend. Four-year-olds use phrases like, "Let's pretend," "You be the doctor," and "Not really real," to indicate their awareness of pretend play. Furthermore, in contrast to younger children who always seem to avoid being the bad guy, fours and fives are more flexible. However, imaginary creatures can still be too frightening to contemplate. Todd loved to play the part of Franken-stein and scare his mother's visitors, but he wasn't too happy about listening to monster records:

> "One record that I have to put up scares me to death. A werewolf makes horrible noises. I'm not listening to that anymore. Not till I'm six—no way."

NEW BUILDING AND DRAWING SKILLS

The building and drawing skills of fours and fives improve dramatically. Children learn to draw forms like the square, the triangle, and the cross. Along with the circle, which appears at an earlier age, they can create pictures of people, buildings, vehicles, flowers, and many other things. This same knowledge of space is applied in three dimensions. Children learn to build block enclosures that become houses and cages. They discover how to make bridges and tunnels by using crossbars. A series of crossbars creates a roof for an enclosure or a building with several stories. With these basic building principles a great variety of structures can be built.

Drawings may lead to imaginative stories, and buildings may lead to extended play with miniature props. On the other hand, a drawing or a building may be an end in itself, a product of the imagination that the child wants to save and admire. In either event the greatly improved construction skills of four- and five-year-old children open up new media for imaginative play.

SEPARATION OF SEXES

A final characteristic of four- and five-year-old play is related to sex identity. At three-years-old girls and boys play together in a very natural way, and the children frequently try out roles associated with the opposite sex. Boys enjoy being mothers and girls like to imitate their fathers. Boys at this age are naturally attracted to the jewelry and makeup of their mothers, and they like to carry purses. Men in our culture usually wear less interesting accessories, which is perhaps why several of the younger girls in our study decided to act out a masculine identity by making themselves a penis.

At four- and five-years-old the children become more rigid about sex identity. A girl is more likely to insist on playing the mother role. At the same time the mother role is extended to other roles that involve nurturing and service. Favorites include waitress, doctor, store clerk, and teacher. In a similar fashion boys insist on being the father in a pretend family, and the father role is extended to other masculine roles.

In many cases it seems that the father's role as a driver is the element most generalized. Fireman, policeman, motorcycle driver, truck driver, paramedic, astronaut—all of these favorite roles among boys empha- size the act of driving.

At four-years-old, and even more at five, same sex groups are forming. Girls play with girls and boys with boys. Sex-related differ- ences are apparent in noise level, tempo, and excitement. Girls' play is likely to be somewhat more relaxed, with a lot of verbal interplay. Boys are often noisier, more aggressive, and their play faster paced.

One way of explaining the differences in play behavior between boys and girls is to focus on parental influence. Many parents encourage girls to play with dolls but become upset when boys join in doll play or try out a feminine role. On the other hand, there were a considerable number of parents we visited who tried to avoid sex typing and were disturbed when their boys rejected dolls. Even when parents go out of their way not to reinforce sex role stereotypes, differences continue to emerge between girl and boy play as children interact with peers.

Unquestionably, the peer group of four- and five-year-olds exerts an influence on sex-typed play behavior. There is a kind of peer culture among preschool children where play themes and games are passed from the older to the younger children. In order to gain peer accep- tance it is essential for a child to play in the same way that the other children are playing. The familiar refrain, "but the other kids are doing it," begins in the preschool years.

As we review the play of four- and five-year-old children, we recognize age-related developments occur in many aspects of imagina- tive play. Peer play has become increasingly important and involves the separation of the sexes. Themes are more varied, elaborate, and cre- ative, and language is used extensively to set the stage and provide continuity. The pretend element is recognized and announced, and the role play involves not only wearing the right costume but taking on other characteristics and actions related to the role.

OBSERVING PLAY STYLES

ACTOR PLAY—Acting is very much a social activity. A child who is acting out a part needs other people, either to be fellow actors or to be an audience. In fact, these two alternatives define fairly distinct kinds of actor play. When other people join in as actors, the play tends to be dominated by the conversation that develops. The pretending is reminiscent of a soap opera in which dialogue amplifies every change in events. When other people play the role of an audience, the child becomes a virtuoso performer, which for preschool children means lots of action and sound effects. We might describe these two kinds of actor play as the conversational actor and the performing artist.

With younger preschool children the conversational actor depends on the adult to maintain the flow of the dialogue. With adults who enjoy role play and are willing to contribute their own creativity and resourcefulness, the performance is fun to watch. Terry and his father provided us with a striking example of conversational acting when they played fireman. Driving to an imaginary fire, they strapped pillows on their backs for oxygen tanks and began to crawl around the living room on their stomachs. Although this action was certainly dramatic, the heart of the pretending lay in their conversation.

Father: I think I'm trapped in the fire.

Terry: No, you're not trapped in the fire. The people are trapped in the fire.

Father: Should we try to rescue them?

Terry: I'm crawling in the fire.

Father: What are you going to do?

Terry: Put them in the ambulance. I'm taking them to the hospital.

Father: What will we do next?

Terry: Well, we have to get the dog out and the mommy and the daddy . . .

Father: We have the fire out.

Terry: Now we have to put the ladder back.

Father: Could we go back to the station and have a cold beer?

Terry: We're back. We're waiting for the next fire. (They pretend to eat and drink.)

As the more mature conversationalist, Terry's father took the responsibility for keeping the dialogue alive. Often he asked a question that stimulated Terry to respond. The question might encourage Terry to describe his actions: "What are you going to do?" The question might suggest a new direction in the play: "Could we go back to the station and have a cold beer?" Whether asking questions or making statements, Terry's father gently led the conversation from one topic to another. Given this framework Terry was able to play out the role of conversational actor. He initiated the idea of a dog, a mommy, and a daddy being trapped in the fire. He described how he was crawling in

Fireman Terry back at the station.

the fire, putting the victims in the ambulance, and controlling the
ladder truck.

In actor-type conversations, the other characters who join in as
fellow actors do not have to be other people. They may be dolls or
stuffed animals. Of course, it is more challenging to carry on a conversation with a doll or stuffed animal as the child needs to speak for
everyone. Usually the child speaks in only one voice, leaving appropriate silences for the comments of the other actor. By listening to the
words of the child, we can infer what the doll is supposed to have said.
In the following example Kori was pretending to wash her doll's hair. At
first she carried on both sides of the conversation, then her role as an
authority figure began to dominate the conversational role, and we have
to imagine the crying and whining of the unhappy doll.

> *Kori:* Okay, I'm going to rinse you now, Alyse. Are you going to
> cry about it?
>
> *Alyse:* No, I won't cry when you rinse me, Kori. Kids don't cry
> when their big sisters rinse them. That's the silliest thing I
> ever heard in the whole wide world.
>
> *Kori:* Alyse, you're crying. I'm just doing the bath. You don't have
> to cry about that. Are you crying about that?
>
> *Alyse:* . . . .
>
> *Kori:* I just have to do the front. Are you crying about that? I'll do
> it fast.

103

Alyse: . . . .

  Kori: You want some buttercup? I'll make you some buttercup. It
will just take one minute. Okay, Alyse, here's your buttercup. Okay?

Children, like Kori, who develop a style of conversational acting
with their dolls, may become proficient enough to sustain two parts at
once. In a school scene involving the puppets Big Bird and Grover, Kori
kept in mind the different perspectives of both the mother (Big Bird)
and the child (Grover). Big Bird was trying to leave her child Grover at
school, while Grover was trying to delay his mother's departure:

Big Bird: I have to go home and make lunch.

  Grover: No, you got to be a parent helper. If you don't be a
parent helper, I'm going to run out of school and never
come back.

Big Bird: You can't run out of school. You go play with Lego
blocks.

  Grover: I hurt my knee. I want a Band-Aid.

Eventually the squabble degenerated into a real fight and Big
Bird, being the parent and therefore stronger, threw Grover to the
floor.

A second type of actor play involves putting on a performance.
Zach provides some good examples. We have already described how he
turned himself into a vacuum cleaner and sucked up an imaginary pie
on the floor and how he turned himself into a birthday present for his
mother by wrapping himself in a sheet. These dramatic transformations
are typical. One of his favorite performances is to play *Star Wars* by
becoming both Luke Skywalker and a rocket ship. Zooming through the
house in a T-shirt of his father's, he seems more rocket ship than space
warrior. A closely related routine is Super Zach with Vampire Bat on his
back. At Halloween Zach and the bat, who is a furry, stuffed frog, hid in
a "vampire box." The audience was supposed to walk by the box and be
suitably frightened when the demonic duo leaped out.

Still another Halloween performance involved a ghost mask. Zach
cut two holes in a paper plate and tried to terrorize his mother by
popping out from behind doors. She told the ghost that it was too early
for Halloween candy, but this information only spurred him on. On
other occasions Zach has been a robot with a paper bag mask, and a
western desperado who orders his mother to "come out with your

Super Zach with vampire bat on his back.

hands up." Zach's mother, who is his primary audience, plays an active role in these pretenses. She must be appreciative, frightened, surprised, and amazed at the appropriate moment.

Sometimes Zach's performance becomes more organized and he is less of a stunt man and more of a performing artist. One unorthodox production centered around the killing of a bug. First Zach showed his mother how to stomp vigorously on an imaginary bug. Then he demonstrated the effect on the poor bug. Lying on his back he shook his legs and made swooshing noises, as if the bug was deflating as it died. More traditional was a twenty-minute concert on the piano and the harmonica, which was inspired by his sister's recital. After each number the audience clapped dutifully, but Zach announced, "Not done yet," in order to keep them in their seats.

When children take on the role of performing artist, music and dance are often selected as the preferred media. We witnessed an elaborate dance routine at Kristine's house. Kristine put on a record about two little elephants who were lost. Obviously she had danced to the record many times already.

As the words were sung, Kristine danced out the story in pantomime. Her style was very vigorous and athletic, like a gymnastic floor exercise. She marched back and forth across the room, bending and bowing from side to side. When the singer spoke of the mother elephant's sadness, Kristine crossed her arms in a hugging gesture. She looked plaintively ahead as the mother elephant searched. She held up two fingers and rhythmically shook them every time the singer repeated the phrase "two little elephants." When the singer suggested that everyone help look for the elephants, she pointed a finger at the audience and jabbed it at them for emphasis.

This style of actor play was highly valued in Kristine's family. Her mother watched with evident pride, and Kristine danced with confidence. Kristine's mother told us that her daughter often danced to songs on records and on television, and that she had started this distinctive style of imaginative play when she was two years old.

PRODUCER-DIRECTOR PLAY

THE SCRIPTWRITER—Just as some children prefer to be actors, other children prefer to express their creativity by directing or producing an imaginary event. There are story tellers, whom we might call the scriptwriters. Although their stories often revolve around their own exploits, the focus is on producing a story rather than acting out a part. Brian, who was an inveterate storyteller, often described a disaster of one kind or another. For example, one day his mother and a friend were discussing the hurricane season in Florida, and he offered the following story:

> "There was a hurricane over the house. A hand came down and picked Brian up by the hair. He cut the hand off, and it fell to the ground. He took the hand to jail."

On another occasion Brian was eating lunch and the subject of robbers came up:

> "The robber is the bad guy because he steals. He is at the top of the ladder, and Big Bear shoots him with a bow and arrow. The robber falls into the street, and a car runs over him, and it squashes him. The eye pops out. The police come and take the robber to jail. The eye had feet and went to jail with the robber. With a bump and a bang, the eye hops back into his head and that's the end."

Just as an actor relies on certain gestures and phrases to create a role, the storyteller falls back on familiar devices. In Brian's stories the drama usually was generated by a monster character. Even a hurricane becomes a monster who can pick up Brian with his hand. As the plot unfolds the villain is laid low by a fearless hero. The hurricane loses its hand, and the robber loses his eye. Then, for good measure, the monster character is put in jail.

Brian also told stories about a paradise of sorts, a farm where he and Danny, his invisible friend, spent the day milking the cows—"first the front and then the back." The farm was a peaceful place where the cows did not bite and the horses took naps. Sometimes the pigs frightened Mr. Lizard, another imaginary friend, with their greediness, but still they were harmless enough.

> "Mr. Lizard wanted to go to the farmhouse with me. He was afraid of the pigs. I saw the pigs eating the hay, and I said to them not to eat the hay. It's for the horses. Then the pigs wanted my peanut butter and jelly sandwich, but I told them they are silly."

Brian's farm is a symbol of harmonious cooperation between people and animals. People feed the animals, and in turn, the animals help the people. The cows in particular are needed to continue the cycle. Brian recounted how once the milk had sprayed on the ground and all the babies had fallen down and died. In contrast to Brian's other stories the farm stands out as an oasis of civilization in an otherwise violent and dangerous world.

THE SONGWRITER—Related to the scriptwriter is the songwriter. Again, children who write songs are in part actors because they perform their own songs, but most of their energy goes into the creation of the song rather than the singing of it. The spontaneous songs of a preschool child may originate as a child is musing out loud and experimenting with the sounds of the words. Kori, for example, thought up the following jingle while riding in the family Honda:

> Hey—sway, get out of Honda's way.
> Isn't that a funny word—hee, hee.

Another song celebrated the joy of taking a walk.

> You can kick with your feet
> when you're walking down the street.
> You can see an Eskimo
> when you're walking with your family.

In these songs Kori tried to capture the rhythm and mood of a daily activity. The songs of preschool children may also explore a new concept. Kori was attracted to the idea that flower bulbs are taken in during the winter and stored in a cool dark place. She made up a song that reflected her way of rationalizing this practice:

Flowers grow in the winter time,
    all day long.
Raggie likes flowers in the winter
    time better.
It's better to put them to sleep.

Frequently preschool children create a song that expands a category of interest. This kind of song may be little more than a listing with
appropriate humming. Erik sang a song called "vegetables." It went like
this: "Cucumbers . . . hmmm, hmmm, Sweet potatoes . . . hmmm, hmmm,
Artichokes . . . hmmm, hmmm," etc. Given help with the structure, the
song may become much more complex. Erik's parents suggested one
day that he start each line with the words, "I wish." With this aid he
produced a song/poem that revealed his strong sense of kinship with
the world of objects:

I wish I was a telephone.
Someone would call me.
I wish I was a big grocery store.
Some people will go in me and buy food.
I wish I was Scotch tape and a box.
Some people would wrap packages to other people—
And it would be me, I wish.
I wish I was a bookcase.
Some people pick books out of me.
I wish I was a real tractor.
A man would ride me and scoop up the dirt
And put it in the dump truck.

THE SET DESIGNER—Another way that some children express their
creativity is by designing a set. Sometimes these set designers specialize
in creating pictures, other times they concentrate on building props.
Drawing and building are related activities. Both involve creating new
forms that can be appreciated by the eye.

Among preschool children, drawing often stimulates pretending
in almost an accidental way. That is, the child sees an imaginary form
after the drawing has been finished. Erik, for example, used water
colors to paint a picture of blobs. One blob accidentally looked like a
turtle, which led to the following story:

"Once upon a time there was a turtle and he swam. And he swam
in the orange water, and the pink water, too. He swam in the
yellow water."

A crayon drawing with isolated scribbles of different colors and a red line produced a similar story:

> "There once was a car that drived on the long highway to visit his grandmother. He stopped at lots of picnic grounds and rest areas—all different colors. He saw lots of grass. And finally he got to his grandmother's."

Much of Kori's drawing was similarly random, but one subject that she worked hard to draw on purpose was a house plan. Her parents were building a house, and Kori was both excited and frightened by the prospect. She constantly was drawing hallways and bathrooms, two of the most important features in her house plan. The drawings were called "mezigns," and one day Kori happily informed the builder of the house, "I built a sun door house, and I 'zined' it myself."

The real burst in representational drawing usually occurs when children are between five- and seven-years-old. Some preschool children, however, have enough drawing skill to pursue a variety of imaginary themes. John hurt his hand at preschool and had to go to the hospital for stitches. Later he drew a picture of a little girl and her father. They were at the hospital because the little girl had cut her hand and the doctor had to sew it up. On another occasion John drew a page full of eyes and commented, "They are looking at me—I like that." His favorite subjects were water creatures, like sharks and alligators. On our visit to his home we watched him draw a detailed killer whale. Trying to catch these animals was a constant theme with John. In the bathtub he was Tarzan and caught alligators by pretending to swim. Outside the bathtub the dog became a shark whose collar could be grabbed. Drawing a picture of a killer whale represented one more way for John to capture a dangerous creature of the sea.

A set designer may choose to use blocks and other building toys to set the stage for pretending. Jad was obsessed with building farmhouses. One of his favorite toys was a farm set, which included some animals, miniature people, and a ready-made barn. Jad decided the animals could sleep in the barn, but the people needed a house. After constructing a farmhouse out of toy bricks, Jad built a garage with irregular walls and an uneven roof. He felt it was imperative for the farmhouse to have a full-fledged garage, in contrast to his own house that had only a carport. Near the barn Jad placed his toy hospital.

Together the farm and the hospital created an imaginary set that held special meaning for Jad. In his play the hospital served as a symbol of family separation. Miniature characters from the farm who were hurt had to be hospitalized, and none of their relatives could visit them:

John and his killer whales.

> You can't come to visit.
> The doctor's still taking X-rays.
> The hurt guy has to sleep. . . .

The relatives were in the same predicament as Jad in real life. He could not visit his father, a resident doctor who worked long hours at a hospital. At night, though, all the hospital personnel, including the patients, traveled to the farm to sleep. Jad's toy farm was a symbol of family togetherness, just like the real farm in Oklahoma where Jad went with his parents to visit relatives.

THE DIRECTOR—Once a set is constructed, the action can begin. The child who has produced the set may now direct the performance. The director role is most apparent when miniature toys are being animated in a pretend scene. The children become omnipotent overseers, manipulating the characters as they see fit. The following scene is typical. We enter the scene as Sheryl is placing a set of miniature people in a dollhouse.

> Okay, Mommy, you go up the stairs.
> One, two, three, four.
> Your turn, baby.
> Want to hide behind the staircase?
> Here's a place for you to hide.
> You get inside, boy—don't go over there.

110

Then it occurs to Sheryl that the boy doll could play on the fence. She starts to sing her directions to the tune of "Farmer in the Dell":

He's walking on the fence,
He's walking on the fence.
Heigh-ho, the derrio,
He's walking on the fence.

No sooner has the family settled down than Sheryl picks up the daddy character:

"The daddy's going in the garage.
He's hammering (bangs the doll against the garage).
He's breaking up the house."

The house turns over and chaos reigns until Sheryl's mother suggests building a school out of blocks. Soon the family is arriving in a schoolbus:

Okay, everybody out of the bus.
Sit in your chairs.
Sing—sing in your seats.
Okay, school's over—out!

The dolls are placed in a line on separate blocks which then suggests a parade to Sheryl. She commands the parade to get organized. Of

Sheryl preparing for the parade.

course, since she is the only worker available, it is up to her to line up the vehicles. These are connected with a piece of twine, and a windup train is placed at the front to lead the procession. Predictably, the train tips over, the knots come apart, and the parade is a general flop. Not discouraged, Sheryl accepts the suggestion that she serve hot dogs to the parade bystanders. When this idea wears thin, there is a car crash that requires sending several characters to the hospital. A good director, like a drill sergeant, may be capricious but is never at a loss for something to do. There are always orders to be issued, work to be assigned.

In describing the play styles of preschool children, we have drawn an analogy between the children and the world of show business. This should not be surprising since show business is, in a sense, an adult version of imaginative play. It seems especially fitting to end our discussion of producer-director play with a show business example. One morning Terry woke up and asked his mother if he could watch "Sesame Street." "It is not on in the morning," she explained and went into her room. When she came back out, she was surprised to find Terry staring intently at a blank wall.

Mother: What are you doing?

Terry: I'm watching "Sesame Street."

Mother: Oh.

Terry: I can't hear very well. I'm going to turn it up (pretends to turn a knob). Can you hear it?

Mother: Yes, I can hear it fine.

Terry: Look, Mom. Ernie has three hats. (Starts to laugh) Isn't he funny?

Mother: Yes, he is.

Terry: Look, Mom, the Cookie Monster and Oscar are fighting.

Mother: Yes, they are.

Terry: "Sesame Street" has been brought to you by the letter "G."

Mother: Is it a capital G or a little g?

Terry: It's a capital "G." Quiet, let's clap. It's all over now. Can I turn it off?

OBSERVING IMAGINATIVE PLAY AT SCHOOL

In our observations of imaginative play in preschool settings we found enormous variability. In academically-oriented schools when the day was fast-paced and highly structured, we saw very little imaginative play. In schools that encouraged discovery learning and creativity, imaginative play was more common. Generally speaking, we found that both the quantity and quality of imaginative play was dependent upon the value system of the staff. When the staff of a school recognized the contributions of imaginative play and fostered its development, imaginative play flourished.

Certain kinds of imaginative play are more suited to a school setting. Usually the play revolves around the peer group because adults do not have time to participate directly. As we have described in earlier chapters, the peer group gets caught up in a pretend version of Follow the Leader. The behavior of a dominant child is copied by other children in the group. Much of the play is concerned with establishing a dominance hierarchy, and for this reason family play is especially popular. The roles of mother, father, child, and baby lend themselves to the expression of dominance or submission. Pretend fighting is also a favored form of imaginative play, especially among boys. Dominance can be asserted through this fighting, or equality can be established by pretending to fight an invisible enemy.

Elaborate solitary play is not common in schools. There is not enough privacy, and special constructions have to be picked up at the end of each day. Children have few if any private possessions in a classroom, which discourages the collection and organization of a large number of props. The more intimate and personal forms of pretending are also rare. There are too many disruptions in a busy classroom, and the attention of supportive adults must be shared with other children. Invisible friends make few appearances; pretending based on extended conversation is unlikely; and pretending that involves the expression of fears is usually not carried out to a point of resolution. Although pretending in a preschool may not be as spontaneous or elaborate as the pretending that takes place at home, a creative teacher can plan an environment where imaginative play can flourish.

The first step in planning how to encourage more imaginative play in a classroom is to observe the spontaneous pretending that is already taking place. One way of simplifying the task is to draw up a list of questions before doing any observation. Answer the questions and then observe the classroom over a two- or three-day period to verify your answers. Here is a list of questions that can serve as a starting point:

1. What are the major play themes that are taking place in the classroom?
2. What pretend roles are the children adopting?
3. What spaces are being used for imaginative play?
4. What props are used most frequently?

The following description of a preschool classroom may help you prepare for your observation. In this particular classroom imaginative play was an important part of the curriculum, and the children responded with a high level of pretending. Imaginative play will not be so pervasive in most classrooms, but similar kinds of activities still will be present.

"Parents' Nursery" is housed in a large one-story building which had once been a combination garage and storehouse. As we enter the building we encounter two boys lying side by side in the middle of an improvised boat.

"Let's get the alligators," one boy shouts as he paddles the boat with his arms.

"I'm the captain," declares the other, raising a foot in the air.

"Water's coming in," the first boy announces as he rearranges some long planks which are serving as the sides of the boat.

Just beyond the boat three boys are attempting to pile up some large wooden boxes. Again, we pick up snatches of a conversation.

"I'm moving this one."

"I'll move it too."

"No, I'm building it myself. I want some privacy. This will be my hideout."

"No, this is my apartment."

"I want to jump."

"You can't jump. It's not sturdy. You'll topple it."

"You have to let him jump. Otherwise, I'll put you in jail."

A red-headed youngster, who calls himself Gonzalez the terrible, insists that we watch him fly. After jumping off the second stair of a playhouse ladder several times, Gonzalez invites a girl named Sue to fly down with him. Sue, who has a towel draped over her shoulders, explains that she is Superwoman and she will jump down on Friday.

Beyond the playhouse we find another group of children very

much involved with kindergarten blocks. One boy has propped a long plank against the wall and is using it as a "ski jump" for his miniature truck. A second child has put together some wooden railroad tracks and is busy building a very long tunnel. A girl, who is watching the tunnel being built, asks how he will get the train out. "I got long arms," the boy explains, stretching his arms in the air. "And anyway, you should know this is an underground, and that's what it is."

> "Fire—fire!! Climb the ladder, man the hose—get the baby—put on your fire hat!"

We turn toward the corner of the room where several children have converged on another two-story block structure. On the lower level of the structure a girl and a boy are shoving a large doll and all of her belongings into a baby carriage. On the upper level two enthusiastic firemen are helping a "family" do something or other with a large shopping bag. It is difficult to sort out exactly what is happening but there is obviously a medical emergency. "Get the shot needle—find the stethoscope! The baby's burning up!!"

In a corner alcove there is a dress-up trunk. One little girl who has been busily rummaging through the trunk, emerges wearing a flimsy pink net costume, and carrying a patent leather purse. "I am Snow White," she announces proudly. "I'm going shopping to buy some lemons."

We follow Snow White into a second alcove where a group of children are listening to a teacher read a story. The teacher has his right hand inside a frog puppet.

> "So Goldilocks took a taste of the little bear's porridge," the teacher reads in a singsong voice. The frog puppet on his right hand interrupts, "I don't think she should have done that. Do you think she should have done that, Micah?"

Micah agrees with the frog, and the teacher continues with the story. We listen to a few more side conversations between the frog and the children and then proceed to the playground.

The playground, like the indoors, is spacious, with clusters of playground equipment suggestive of different imaginative themes. Beside an animal cage area where a boy is feeding an imaginary tiger, there is a growing pit with garden tools, a merry-go-round, a trolley, two tree stumps with steering wheels and two rather elaborate climbing structures. Several children are making their way across parallel ladders, throwing torpedoes at the sharks that are swimming in the ocean below.

"We killed all the sharks," shouts a tall boy triumphantly, but his friend discovers a hundred-teen more and the torpedo throwing starts again.

The two friends find a second structure that is a fine height for jumping.

"We are both birds."
"We fly."
"We are both birds, right. Going flip-flop."

At this point, one of the teachers realizes that the morning too has flown by and summons the children in for cleanup time. The teacher compliments the children on how beautifully they cleaned up the room. "Who did the cleanup jobs?" he asks. "Who did three? Who did four?" Everyone, of course, raises a hand in response to each of the questions. After some urging by the children, the parent helper sings several rounds of a "Little Bunny Foo Fan" song, and the children sing the chorus. "What did you do this morning?" one of the mothers asks as she picks up her son. "Nothing," he explains, " 'cept I played and I ate up the crust on my peanut butter sandwich."

FROM THE LITERATURE

In their book, *Children Tell Stories*, Evelyn Pitcher and Ernst Prelinger analyze a large collection of stories told by children between the ages of two and five.° Their comparison of boys' and girls' stories suggests how a child's perception of the world is shaped by sex roles.

Stories by boys revolve around occupational roles, vehicles, and animals. Violence is prominent in that the animals are wild, the occupations are dangerous, and the vehicles get smashed. Boys understandably show more concern in their stories over being attacked and hurt. However, when a character dies, it usually is an animal rather than a person. Death is often the result of aggression.

Girls mention parents more frequently in their stories, and they express more hostility toward mother figures. Fictional characters are more likely to be given a name and personality. Friendship and marriage appear in their stories. The most common form of aggression is spanking, which occurs because a child character has committed some minor infraction. When death appears in a story it is usually the result of illness rather than violence.

Pitcher and Prelinger's analysis supports the general view that

°Evelyn Pitcher and Ernst Prelinger, *Children Tell Stories* (New York: International University Press, 1969).

boys are more oriented toward achievement in the world outside their home. Girls focus on interpersonal relationships, girls include characters of both sexes in their stories. A character may even change back and forth from one sex to another. Boys, on the other hand, rarely include female characters in their stories. In their eyes the world of achievement is male-dominated.

Chapter Five

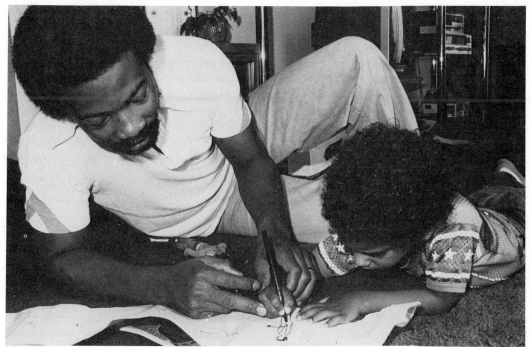

The Adult
as Planner
How parents and teachers
can set the stage for pretending

Although young children can develop a pretend theme without toys or other props, the quality of their pretending is enhanced when adults set up the environment. Setting the stage for pretending requires both planning the play space and selecting props with the appropriate blend of realism and versatility. In a larger sense, it involves building a foundation of real world experiences that fills children with joy, wonder, and excitement. Experience that surprises and delights a child is the wellspring of creativity and the inspiration of imaginative play. In the first section of this chapter, we discuss how parents can promote imaginative play at home. In the second section, we look at the same planning process within a preschool classroom.

SETTING THE STAGE AT HOME

PROVIDE A PLACE TO PRETEND—Much of the early pretending that children do is based on imitation. When children imitate the actions of other people, the best place for pretending is where the action normally occurs. The sink in the kitchen is where you pretend to wash dishes, the workbench suggests pretending to fix things, the closet is the place for dressing up.

Pretending that is less imitative calls for its own special place. Often children look for a small enclosed space that can become a home, a vehicle or a hideaway. Michael's favorite spot was a kitchen cupboard which his mother helped him empty out. For several weeks "choo-choo" noises emanated from the cupboard as Michael took off on his daily train ride to California.

A large cardboard box is another good enclosure for pretending. Most of the time children will use a large box as a playhouse, but it can have other uses. Karis and Stacy found a box with a hole in it and turned it into a television set. They put a stick through the side of the box and attached Tinkertoy "knobs" to it, so the set could be turned on and the channel changed. From inside the box, Karis performed songs that she associated with favorite television shows. On another channel an abbreviated news show was offered: "And now the weather—it's going to snow."

In most instances preschool children prefer a pretend play space that is in the center of the action. A box in the kitchen, living room, or family room is used more than a box left in a bedroom or outside. For the same reason, upholstered furniture in the center of a sitting area is especially popular for pretending. Chad's favorite spot, for example, was a large chair in the living room. On our visit to his home the chair became a fort in which Chad hid from us with several stuffed animals: Pooh Bear, Kermit the Frog and Donkey. Later the fort caught on fire.

"I have to get everything out," Chad muttered, throwing animals right and left. "The fireman has to come in here—come right inside." Extinguishing the fire with the usual sound effects, Chad then settled back in the chair with his friends: "Climb aboard—back into the fort. We have to go home."

"Sit down on my riding couch," Laura invited her mother. Like Laura, many children adopt the couch as a special place for pretending. The couch itself makes a good train or airplane; while couch cushions can be used to build tents, garages, or clubhouses. In lieu of cushions several families we visited provided their children with large pillows for building pretend spaces. David, when pretending to go on a safari, used a set of pillows with a floral pattern to simulate a jungle. Later he gathered the pillows together and built a cage for wild animals and a jail for his sister. A beanbag chair represents a kind of pillow that stimulates pretending. It may serve as a bed or a swimming pool. In Zach's case a beanbag chair even became a turtle shell. Placing the bright yellow beanbag on his back, he crawled slowly around the room in authentic turtle fashion.

As preschool children become older and increasingly able to organize and sustain imaginative play by themselves, there is a growing tendency to construct imaginary play spaces. This construction often involves extensive moving of furniture and rearrangement of cushions. Sometimes children can be convinced to move their grandiose projects to more remote parts of the house. This gives them more freedom to rearrange things and a greater degree of privacy. Scott and his six-year-old brother were encouraged to do most of their pretending in the basement. There the furniture could be turned into a wagon train or a pirate ship and could stay that way for as long as they wanted.

The desire for more privacy in pretending emerges sporadically with four- and five-year-olds. They do not like to be pushed into pretending away from the center of the family's activity. In several situations we saw pretending decline when parents provided more privacy than the children really wanted. As a two-year-old, Brian's favorite place to play was a plywood fort that his parents had built in the family room. Brian climbed the walls, hid inside the fort, and used the window to conduct pretend conversations with his parents. A year later Brian's parents moved the fort outside, thinking it would stimulate a greater variety of pretend themes. Instead, Brian played less in the fort and his pretending was channeled into storytelling. Telling stories kept him in the center of the family circle, while playing in the fort was too far out on the periphery.

Robbie's parents made a similar mistake when they tried to move

Brian in his fort.

his pretending to the garage. Robbie was getting older and had accumulated stacks of toys. The empty garage, which had built-in storage bins, seemed the ideal place. Regrettably, moving the toys outside led to a decline in pretending. Robbie stopped pretending in the house because all his toys were gone and he didn't like pretending in the garage because it was too far away.

Robbie's case illustrates the value in letting children find their own spaces for pretending. Every home and every yard offers different possibilities. A central hall may stimulate pretend deliveries. A linen closet full of extra cosmetics may become a drugstore where children shop. An extra-wide window sill, or an oversize closet, may become a miniature environment just right for accommodating the imaginative play of preschool children.

Whatever the space for pretending, parents need to anticipate considerable messiness and some chance of property damage. Imaginative play is not a neat undertaking. When Zach built a tent house, it was filled to the brim as he attempted to move into his new quarters. In the same way Darrius built a version of the Orange Bowl parade that included every toy in his bedroom. A good idea tends to be pushed as far as it will go and to occupy as much space as possible.

MAKE PLAY MATERIALS AVAILABLE—Just as real spaces are often appropriated for pretend events, real objects are prized as imaginative props. The typical home is a virtual gold mine of play materials for the preschool pretender.

122

BABY EQUIPMENT—Baby equipment, which the child has so recently outgrown, is invaluable in acting out a parent role. Dolls can be fed in a high chair, put to sleep in a cradle, or taken shopping in a stroller.

CLOTHES—Clothes of all kinds are good for imaginative play. Baby clothes can be put on stuffed animals or dolls. Adult clothes can be tried on for size and packed in a suitcase. Often the dressup outfits of preschool children are not elaborate. A tie around the neck may make the child a businessman, a fur hat may be sufficient for visiting the North Pole. Amy used a particular belt to create a variety of characters. Wearing the belt around her middle, she became Spiderman; with the belt around her head she was an Indian.

TOOLS—Tools are another category of real objects that children like to use when pretending. Although some tools are too dangerous for young children to handle, others are very suitable. A paintbrush and a bucket of water is perfect for painting the outside of the house or sidewalk. A rubber hammer is ideal for pounding on a durable toy, like a tricycle or a wagon. Tools may be used in new ways too. A small air pump makes a good hypodermic needle, a plumber's helper can be a versatile steering wheel, a spray bottle full of water can be used to make rain.

KITCHEN OBJECTS—Pretend cooking is more exciting with real objects from the kitchen, especially objects that children are not free to use under normal circumstances. A set of hot pads, for example, which usually is reserved for adult use, makes pretend dishes from the oven

Kitchen props.

seem especially hot. A real rolling pin improves pretend pie crusts. A baster is good for seasoning a pretend Thanksgiving turkey.

The appeal of a real object may even extend to an empty container. An empty cocoa can, an empty salt box, or an empty catsup bottle is close enough to the real thing to bring out a child's fantasies. The key to a prop's success is its emotional value to the child. An empty cake mix box is likely to have more impact than an empty oatmeal box, an empty beer can generally stimulates more imaginary thirst than an empty orange juice can.

Traveling themes are enriched by objects like an old suitcase, a real map, and a set of real keys. Pretend shopping is more fun with props like wrapping paper, old credit cards, and green stamps. The possibilities for incorporating real objects into pretend situations is endless. The only limitations are that the objects should be safe, and not too messy or too valuable to use for pretending.

TOYS—Toys, of course, have a role in pretending. In deciding what toys to buy for imaginative play, the child's interests will be the primary consideration. A child who is fascinated by the garbage truck will pretend a great deal with a toy garbage truck, especially if it is large enough to put some "garbage" inside. A child who likes to watch paramedics on television is likely to treasure a toy ambulance or fire truck.

There also are some general considerations to keep in mind. Many children already have a variety of dolls, stuffed animals, trucks and cars. For these children a different type of toy might inspire more pretend play. A toy that can take the place of a real object is one possibility. For example, a set of play dishes is especially appropriate if a family does not have any unbreakable dishes that can be used for pretending. A play telephone is worth purchasing if the real phone is off limits. Another possibility is a toy that provides a prop which is hard to create at home. A doctor's kit, if it is a quality toy, is a good idea because suitable substitutes for a stethoscope or a blood pressure cuff are hard to find around the house. A shopping cart may be a good investment if a stroller or other substitute is not available.

The best toys for imaginative play are those that can be used in many different ways over a period of years. A set of long blocks are especially useful for roads, bridges, fences, railroad tracks, and buildings. Smaller blocks, in different colors and shapes, complement the larger building blocks. They can be used to decorate the outside of a building or to make furniture and mosaic floors inside the building. Blocks or sticks that can be connected together are good for creating props. Large plastic pop beads are especially versatile. Connected together, a string of beads can become a crown, a belt, or a gun. Used separately, the beads serve as trinkets or money. Laura even used the beads to play "makeup", a favorite theme with several children:

Laura: Here's your yellow lipstick (rubbing the tip of a yellow bead across her mother's mouth). Oops! Got some on your teeth.

Mother: How about some hair spray?

Laura: Orange, here's hair spray.

Mother: That's enough. Want to feel it? It makes my hair stiff.

Laura: (Holding a new bead) This is a Q-tip for your fingernails.

Mother: You forgot my toes.

Many new playscapes have been marketed for young children in recent years. By playscapes we mean miniature environments for pretending, such as an airport, a McDonald's restaurant, a treehouse, etc. Along with the playscape comes a variety of miniature characters, furniture, and other accessories. For some children, especially four- and five-year-olds, these toys do stimulate imaginative play. In most cases, children enjoy playing with the accessories to a playscape more than the playscape itself. They like to use the miniature accessories in different settings, rather than being limited to the ready-made one.

We do not mean to suggest that playscapes are undesirable toys, but only that adults should evaluate them carefully. If a preschool child can build his own version of an airport, a restaurant, or a dollhouse, it seems best to concentrate on providing that child with a rich supply of accessories. The accessories may include larger vehicles with room for miniature dolls and furniture. A camper, boathouse, or airplane is flexible enough to be incorporated into a variety of pretend themes.

There also are numerous mechanical and electrical toys available for young children. In general these toys do not stimulate a high level of pretending because the child's attention is focused on learning how to operate the toy. A cash register, for example, usually produces less elaborate pretending than a cash box. A toy telephone that includes a toy Jack-in-the-box stimulates fewer pretend conversations than a simpler phone. Furthermore, a mechanical or electrical toy may encourage young children to take a passive role. Instead of actively incorporating the toy into their own pretend ideas, the children stand back and watch the toy perform. Once the toy breaks and can no longer perform, it is likely to be ignored.

Again, we do not want to imply that mechanical or electrical toys are unsuitable for imaginative play. In an earlier chapter we described how Chad created first an office and then a spaceship with this kind of toy. He especially liked to use a siren toy and a play drill to fix his office equipment, and he used the same devices to fix people when he pretended to be a doctor. In this instance, Chad had gone beyond the typical use of these toys. When a mechanical or electrical toy can be used in a variety of ways, or when children impose their ideas on the toy rather than the other way around, this kind of toy can add a new sense of excitement to imaginative play.

Many of the best toys are homemade, not because there is a special virtue in homemade things, but because toys can be tailored to fit the personal interests of an individual child. These homemade toys may be created out of materials that are inexpensive or would be thrown away. Kori, for example, used a soda bottle as Calamine lotion and a catsup bottle as shampoo. Her doll, Alyce, needed one or the other of these bottles nearly every day, and Kori made sure that Alyce got the right one. Zach enjoyed fishing with a stick and a string. Erik pretended to cross a bridge and go to the beach by walking across a board resting on two piles of books. Scott sang songs into a microphone made from the electric skillet cord. Laura pretended to bowl by rolling a ball over some pennies she had arranged on the floor.

Such spur-of-the-moment toys are an integral part of the pretend experience. It is a creative act for children or adults to design their own toys for imaginative play. Adults can help children by keeping an eye out for interesting junk and salvaging it before it is thrown away. Empty containers of all kinds are potential props. Old greeting cards, catalogs, and other printed material may suggest pretend themes.

The most important thing adults can do is to be open to new toy ideas, both their own and those of their children. Acts of inspiration cannot be predicted, but they can be accepted. Chad, for example, put three large paint cans on the front porch and announced they were logs that he was selling. Zach wrapped soap in a washcloth and stuck his hand out of the shower, "Here Mommy, here's a present." To be successful, new ideas like these must receive a response. Chad needed a customer to buy his logs. Zach needed to see his mother's reaction when she opened up her slippery present.

ORGANIZING PLAY MATERIALS

Pretending is easier when play materials are organized. The most natural form of organization is to arrange play materials according to play spaces. Some toys are more suitable for outside play, some for inside. Some materials are appropriate for quiet activities in a living room or bedroom. Others encourage wilder play and usually are found in a recreation room, basement, or garage.

Parents who are so inclined can extend this natural form of organization by thinking about the kind of pretending that their children might enjoy in different spaces. Consider the bathtub as an example. Children who like to play with cars might enjoy driving cars underwater and creating water accidents. Children who pretend to travel might like to take a set of miniature characters on a trip in a boat made out of a cake pan. Children who are involved in pretend cooking could pour out imaginary food and drink in the bathtub with measuring cups and unbreakable dishes. Doll play could be extended in the bathtub to include teaching a doll to swim, washing a doll's hair, or laundering doll clothes. Children attracted to superhero/monster play could be provided with plastic animals and superhero dolls for the bathtub. Often children come up with ideas like these by themselves, but parents can offer additional suggestions. They can also help children store favorite play materials in a convenient place in the bathroom, so they can be located easily next time.

Young children spend much of their time in the kitchen. An obvious pretend theme for the kitchen is cooking. If a child has a pretend stove or refrigerator, it can be placed in the kitchen. Playdough, which many parents avoid because it gets into carpets, is an excellent play material for the kitchen. As parents bake or cut up food, children can pretend to do the same thing with playdough, and any mess that results can be removed from a kitchen floor without too much trouble. Often parents talk on a telephone in the kitchen. If this is the case, a toy telephone mounted on a kitchen wall may lead to an increase in imaginary phone calls. Blocks are another possible play material for the kitchen. Preschool children, especially younger ones, look for the support of an admiring audience when they build. In the kitchen parents can encourage a child's efforts while accomplishing their regular housework.

Another space in which young children find themselves confined is the car. One way parents can respond to the restlessness of a bored child is to provide materials for pretending. For younger preschool children a steering wheel toy allows them to participate in the driving process on an imaginary level, or the children may want to bring along their own purse, keys, shopping list, etc. Older preschool children may enjoy looking at a map. A homemade book might be created with map sections on different pages. Interspersed between the maps could be pictures of interest to the child—relatives, animals, different forms of recreation, and famous places. Given a pencil, the child can trace imaginary routes on the map and pretend to visit the people and places pictured in his travel guide.

Because movement is restricted in the car, it is a good space to encourage the kind of pretending involved in storytelling and story listening. Picture books can be kept in the car for children to look at by themselves. A slide viewer is an excellent car toy because children can utilize the light from the windows and enjoy a quiet, private form of pretending. Certain puppets may be reserved just for pretend conversations and stories in the car. Like Oscar the Grouch, who lives in a garbage can, their permanent home can be in the glove compartment or under the seat.

Whatever space children frequent, adults can set the stage for pretending by providing play materials appropriate to that space. We found that in many of the homes where children pretended the most, parents also had organized play materials along logical lines. Miniature props, such as animals, furniture, people, and vehicles, had been sorted into separate categories and stored in small boxes. In the same way, building materials of various kinds were kept distinct. This kind of logical organization is needed when particular toys exist in abundance. Otherwise children become discouraged looking for the materials they want and imaginative play diminishes. By the same token, play materials that are logically organized invite children to pretend. Preschool children are capable of categorizing toys by themselves, but they do not maintain this kind of order unless adults help them.

Logical organization can be extended beyond obvious categories like animals, vehicles, etc. Materials can be grouped into thematic categories. For example, an old suitcase can be filled with hats, gloves, ties, jewelry, scarves and other dress-up materials. These props all are associated with the theme of pretend traveling. The suitcase serves as both a storage container and an important prop. Doctor play is another theme that lends itself to this kind of organization. A box can be filled with things like a play stethoscope, Band-Aids, tongue depressors, rags for bandages, and empty pill bottles. Better yet, these materials can be placed in a tote bag or old purse that becomes a doctor's bag.

Parents may organize a prop carton for playing fireman, policeman, mechanic, grocery store clerk, or any other role that children are especially interested in acting out. We watched Jamie pretend to make "seven grain cereal" with a collection of bowls, spoons, and the empty food containers that were kept in a large box. Jamie laboriously poured the imaginary contents from one bowl to another, keeping track of which bowls were empty and which were full. As he mixed together lecithin, yeast, and milk, he commented, "I'm sorry, Mom. You can't

Jamie's seven-grain cereal.

have any—it's not good for you." The invisible mixture was stirred with a wooden spoon and tasted very carefully. Finally Jamie added some cotton and rocks to give substance to his cereal and then pretended to eat it. Throughout this scene Jamie was able to concentrate on his pretend ideas because all the materials he needed were close at hand in his "cooking box."

Organization is easier when play materials are limited. Both parents and children benefit when some of a child's toys are put up, out of sight and out of reach. Children can focus their attention more easily in a room that is not cluttered with play materials, and when it is time to pick up, the job is not so overwhelming. There is more space in which to pretend, and imaginary environments tend to stay intact longer. Most important, play materials can be rotated when children become bored with the ones that are available. Parents always have something different to offer their children, and since the children have not played with these materials for some time, they usually see the toys in a fresh light and discover new ways to use them.

Rotating play materials is a flexible process governed by common sense. Favorite toys may never be put up, while other toys may be rotated frequently because children seem to lose interest quickly. No materials are off limits. If children want to play with a toy that has been put up, they need only request it. Like any kind of organization, rotation of play materials takes extra time, but the additional playtime that is generated makes it well worth the effort.

SETTING THE STAGE IN CLASS

Space and play materials are organized in most preschool classrooms according to interest centers. Many classrooms set aside a special place for imaginary play, such as a playhouse, but in reality pretending can take place anywhere in the classroom. We will begin by looking at ways to set the stage in a playhouse and then proceed to other typical interest centers.

The most traditional area for encouraging play within a classroom is the housekeeping center. In many of the classroom areas we found a housekeeping area equipped with a child-size stove, sink, dish cabinet, refrigerator, table and chair sets, and doll cradles. This is a good start, but in order to take full advantage of this very expensive equipment you may want to make some additions. (As you make these additions, keep in mind the themes that interest your children.) It is usually better to have a collection of props relating to one particular theme than to attempt to develop a variety of themes with just one or two props for each.

THE COOKING THEME—Pots and pans, mixing utensils, a chef's hat, apron, sponge and dishcloth, colander, flour sifter, coffee maker, recipe book, pencil and paper, measuring cups, pretend ingredients (large buttons or rocks work well because they make noise when mixed).

THE SERVING FOOD THEME—A tablecloth, a tea set, eating utensils, napkins, candlesticks, a flower centerpiece, a picnic basket.

THE CHILD CARE THEME—Baby bottles, sheets, pillow, blankets, bib, high chair, baby doll, doll diapers and clothes, nurse's and doctor's kit, telephones.

THE RESTAURANT THEME—Menus, pad and pencil, purse, wallet, cash register, aprons, a tray.

Many housekeeping centers include dress-up materials. Standard equipment for this area includes a variety of hats, shirts, skirts, shoes, capes, and dresses.

To encourage "parent" role play add the following props: a mirror, purses, suitcases, wallets, credit cards, play money, old watches and jewelry, lunch boxes, briefcases, play camera, newspapers and magazines.

For additional role play, add firefighter hats, hoses, sirens, sheriff sets, barber shop and beauty shop tools, laundry equipment, tool sets, and camping equipment.

Rather than placing all of the props in the classroom at one time, keep the props for each type of role play in its own prop box and bring out the box in accordance with curriculum objectives or in response to the spontaneous interests of the children.

BLOCK CENTER

The block area is natural for imaginative play. Ready-made structures, like factories, churches, and houses, can be used in combination with regular blocks to create particular scenarios. Children can be encouraged to build neighborhoods. Miniature toy people, objects, and cars can be used to develop activities like going to a restaurant, picking up garbage, or delivering newspapers. Tape can be put on the floor to make roads, ponds, and railroad tracks. Road signs and wooden trees add interesting variations. Barnyards can be created by building pens and farmhouses with blocks and adding miniature animals. One very creative teacher painted railroad tracks, roads, bridges, farmyards and animal cages on a bed sheet. This not only produced a most interesting building stimulus but also kept the block play within a well defined space.

Imaginative building possibilities are virtually unlimited. The periodic addition of new materials keeps the play alive. There are many "junk" materials that can be added to the block area to extend play. These include egg cartons, buttons, packing materials like blocks of foam or styrofoam, cigar and cardboard boxes.

LANGUAGE AND MATH CENTERS

Although language and math centers are often thought of as the "academic" areas of the classroom, the addition of imaginative play both increases their appeal and enhances learning.

In the language center an all-purpose office can be created, with an electric typewriter, filing cabinet, desk, and bulletin board. This office forms an imaginary environment for practicing activities that promote writing and phonics skills. For example, word banks can be filed in the filing cabinet under each child's name; pictures can be filed under their beginning sound; scrapbooks can be made at the desk; names and simple stories can be typed by the children on the typewriter.

In the same way, the math center can be complemented by an all-purpose store environment. Props might include a shelf for displaying merchandise, price stickers, play money and blank checks, a cash register, a small pad for receipts, green stamps, signs that say "For Sale," "Open," and "Closed," a shopping cart, and shopping bags. The all-purpose store can sell any kind of merchandise, as well as being a bank or post office. As the children buy and sell items, there will be many opportunities to count and to categorize. The important thing is to limit the amount of merchandise and to keep it simple so that the children can keep the store organized.

THE PLAY-GROUND

Out-of-doors is an ideal environment for imaginative play to take place. Running space encourages monster play, cops and robbers, and other pretend themes that involve chase and capture. Other types of pretend play can be encouraged by the development of play structures and the addition of appropriate props.

A sandbox represents an easily built play structure that adds many possibilities for imaginative play. A logical theme in the sandbox is "superhighway." The children can build roads and add props like miniature road signs, rest stops, toll booths, a police station, gas station, and hospital. Rocks, sticks, and blocks can be used to build these details. A second theme might be animal environments. All kinds of animals can be used to stimulate environments, like the farm, the zoo, the mountains, desert, swamp, etc. Depending on the props that are made available, a sandbox also can be a gold mine, a cement factory, or a bakery.

Water adds to the appeal of a sandbox, especially if there is a water table nearby or some other large container in which water can be stored. By itself, the water table can be used as a cooking center, a bathtub, a pond for sailing boats, a car wash, or a laundry center.

Small playground spaces that can be used as playhouses, forts, or secret hideaways are important. These spaces are especially appealing if they are built off the ground—on top of a platform or climbing structure. Concrete conduit pipes provide fun hiding spaces. Again, the kind of play that takes place within these structures is influenced by the addition of props. Hats, belts, capes, walking sticks, whistles, blankets, dolls, and stuffed animals can be used to encourage thematic development.

Two themes that are quite popular with preschoolers are the fix-it theme and the gas station theme. These themes are encouraged by a circular pathway for riding tricycles, with perhaps a little hill or a bridge along the pathway. A post with a piece of hose attached to it can serve as a gas pump, and a pulley and hook can be set up for raising "broken" vehicles. Other appropriate props include nonmetal tools (rubber and wooden mallets, plastic screwdrivers and wrenches), paint brushes and cans of colored water, empty gas cans for vehicles out of gas, empty oil cans, and a rope for towing vehicles.

An alternate kind of structure for transportation is a larger, fixed vehicle, like an old boat or car body. An interesting vehicle can be created by attaching a steering wheel to a jungle gym or a tree stump.

BUILDING A FOUNDATION FOR IMAGINATIVE PLAY

Pretending rests on a foundation of real experience. Although children fulfill their wishes and project their fears through pretending, these feelings are usually expressed within a context of reality. The children recreate the world as they know it. The depth and variety of a child's pretending is directly related to the wealth of that child's real world experience. Real world experience sets the stage for later pretending.

Parents and other adults do not need to provide real experience for young children. It is inevitable and inescapable. They can, however, enrich this experience by their behavior. One thing adults can do is to help young children become actively involved in an experience. Children learn a great deal through observation, but they learn even more by actively participating. Generally children do not need to be urged to join in. They have a strong drive to do more than watch from the sidelines. Yet it sometimes takes patience and ingenuity to find a way for young children to participate in our everyday activities.

Grocery shopping is an example of a routine activity in which young children can participate. Naturally, inviting the participation of a youngster can prolong a shopping excursion. At the same time it can turn a tedious chore into an adventure for both child and parent. Parents find that children enjoy shopping more when they are involved from the beginning. Children can help develop a shopping list by looking for missing items on the pantry shelf or by talking with parents about what is planned for dinner. Once in the store, children can push the cart and help to find the way to the different departments. It is amazing to watch how quickly children familiarize themselves with the basic layout of a supermarket. Even a three-year-old will laugh at the idea of searching for a watermelon in the cereal section or looking for a broom in the freezer. Once children have helped you find the correct department, they can also have limited choices in the selection of items. You may let them choose the type of cereal they like or ask them to pick out their favorite can of soup.

If we do take the time to involve children in grocery shopping, their natural interest in ideas related to food will be stimulated. Some of a young child's strongest likes and dislikes center around food. Eating food is a major social event and is the means of growing bigger, a mysterious and exciting prospect. Different kinds of food are associated with holidays and various ethnic groups. Some animals eat strange foods like grass or garbage, and all animals are part of a complex food chain in which one animal eats another. Such notions about food are dawning in the minds of preschool children, and the grocery store, with its thousands of different items, provides a natural focal point for further exploration.

When children and adults share a real experience like grocery shopping, it is not a silent process. Participation leads to conversation, and a large part of the experience lies in the back and forth exchange of ideas. Picking out apples may provoke comments about the physical characteristics of the apples, where they come from, or how they can be used in cooking. Giving a child some choice in buying cereal may lead to a discussion of prices or an argument about the value of sugar in the diet.

As is the case with almost any topic, adults are in a position to dominate a conversation about grocery shopping. They have the knowledge that results from years of participating in this activity. They can point out many ideas that will be new to a young child, such as the fact that frozen food is hard, that different foods are made from milk, that many foods are sold by weight. Such ideas are fine and good if the child is interested in them. If the child is not interested, though, the conversation becomes one-sided and the child's sense of participation suffers.

The most reliable way to tell if children are really participating in a conversation is to listen to their comments and to answer their questions. Simply listening and responding sounds easy, but sometimes it is the hardest thing to do because we are bursting with knowledge that we want to impart to a child. It is natural for us to take the role of a teacher in our conversations with young children, and children look to adults to provide new information, but often our enthusiasm interferes with a child's need to participate.

Sometimes the conversation is virtually the whole experience, as when we talk to children while riding in the car, eating a meal, or tucking them in at night. It is at such times that difficult questions about life and death seem to be raised by children, that speculation about remote and abstract topics is most likely. Children ask about faraway places, and they wonder where the sun goes at night. They want to know whom they will marry, and what happens after a person dies. Questions like these refer to events that are beyond a child's immediate experience but talking about them provides a vicarious substitute.

Vicarious experiences are especially stimulated by books and television. Reading a story or watching a television program is by definition an imaginative experience, for it is the power of imagination that

A serious conversation.

provides a sense of reality. Perhaps that is why we observed few instances in our study in which a story from a book or television program reappeared in pretending. The way to recreate these imaginative experiences is to read the book again or to watch a rerun on television, and this is exactly what young children like to do.

Even though there is little direct copying of a story or television plot, these vicarious experiences do supply new ideas for pretending. The conflicts between cowboys and Indians, or between cops and robbers, are replaced by fights between space warriors and aliens, or between superheroes and evil geniuses. Pretending to drive a car involves jumping obstacles, crashing through roadblocks, and talking on a C.B. radio.

Television seems to be more potent than books in introducing new characters and formats into imaginative play. Perhaps television has more entertainment appeal, or maybe it is simply because children watch television more than they read books. However, we suspect that the impact of television is superficial. Although preschool children have some understanding of the plots they see on television, most of these stories do not speak to their imaginative world. For example, stories about superheroes invariably involve villains who are trying to take over the world through technological wizardry. Preschool children are not afraid of things like mind control or laser weapons, and therefore the plot resolution makes little sense to them. The achievements of the superheroes are appreciated only on a physical level, i.e., superheroes are superstrong, can jump higher, run faster, and swim farther than other people. The children's imaginative play reflects this level of comprehension. As we have described in earlier chapters, pretend superheroes do little more than jump around and make lots of noise.

An example of a television program that does inspire detailed pretending is "Emergency One," a program about paramedics. The program speaks to real fears of preschool children: fires, car wrecks, and people dying from medical emergencies. As a result, children who faithfully watch the program come to understand the actions of the heroes well enough to recreate them in imaginative play.

Books may not be as powerful an influence on young children but they are a more flexible medium. Adults can provide children with books that complement their imaginative play. There are excellent books about children (usually animal children) being separated from their parents, about children getting into trouble with their parents because they are slow, clumsy, or messy. There are stories about making friends and having dangerous adventures. Most of these books can be found in public libraries, and professionals are available to help parents and other adults select specific stories.

Helping select television programs and books for young children is a valuable way to enrich their experience. Even more important is the conversation that accompanies a story or television show. Conversation is both a way of participating more actively in a vicarious experience and a means of sharing that experience with another person.

A preschool, like a home, provides a rich array of opportunities for building a foundation for imaginative play. Although the teacher cannot provide as many opportunities for participation in adult activities as the parent, the classroom has its own advantages. Its special advantage is that each child has contact with a variety of other children. Like other kinds of experience, this social experience is enhanced when filtered through the medium of conversation. Teachers can help children interpret and accept their experience with peers by talking with them about it. Again, there is a danger of overdoing it, but this pitfall should not deter teachers from getting involved in the social interaction of the children. Young children appreciate a teacher's help in trying to understand the behavior of their peers.

A preschool classroom or child care center can also offer children some special experiences. New people, new places, and new ideas can be introduced through field trips. For young children the most rewarding trips are familiar places revisited: the supermarket, the bank, the post office, the kitchen of a fast food restaurant, the airport, the library, a gas station or even a laundromat. Whatever the place, the critical element is the quality of human contact, ensuring that the children meet people who have the time and interest to talk with them.

As an alternative to field trips where the children go out into the community, the community can come into the classroom. Again, teachers need to take into account the point of view of a child when inviting classroom visitors. A telephone repairman who will let the children explore his tool kit, play with wires, and dial a dummy telephone, is a better choice than a lawyer. Other possibilities for classroom visitors include plumbers, electricians, television repairmen, artists, and photographers. When given opportunities to discover the kinds of work that adults perform, children will reenact their discoveries in a pretend routine and gain new understanding about the meaning of work.

Whether at home or at school children's pretending is enriched when the adult provides a foundation of real world experiences. Sometimes we can take a child on a special excursion or plan an exciting event. At other times we can enrich the child's pretending by talking about a routine experience in a way that makes it new. Adults who are interested in enriching the imaginative play of young children do not have to spend money on elaborate toys or plan for exotic experiences. By taking time to tell about the small things that are happening around us, we expand the horizons of children and build a base for pretending.

FROM THE LITERATURE

The effect of television on children is a subject of concern to many teachers and parents. A series of studies have demonstrated rather conclusively that when children watch a violent film, the immediate effect is an increase in aggressive behavior. The converse has also been shown, that watching a program like "Mister Rogers" increases cooperative behavior. Jerome and Dorothy Singer have argued that the rapid pace of television also inhibits the development of imaginative play.[*]

In order to test this theory the Singers asked the parents of 141 preschool children to keep records of their children's television viewing habits. The parents recorded the amount and kind of program watched and the intensity of involvement during four two-week periods over the course of a year. The children were observed at school

[*]Jerome Singer and Dorothy Singer, "Television Viewing and Imaginative Play in Preschool; A Developmental and Parent Intervention Study," Progress Report no. 2 (New Haven: Yale University, May 1978).

during these same two-week periods. Altogether each child's free play was observed eight times during the year, for ten minutes each time.

Contrary to their expectations the Singers found no relationship of statistical significance between television watching and imaginative play. Apparently, watching television neither increases nor decreases the likelihood of pretending. There was a weak pattern that suggested children who pretend the most prefer to watch cartoons, situation comedies, and educational television, while children who pretend less tune into more detective and game shows.

The Singers also tried several parent training programs designed to reduce the amount of watching by young children. One group of parents was given instruction in how to stimulate imaginative play, under the assumption that more pretending would mean less television. A second group was given information about the harmful effects of television and ways were suggested for monitoring and limiting a child's viewing. The results of these training programs were negligible, although the Singers conclude that imaginative play training is more effective than teaching parents direct techniques for altering their children's watching habits.

The Singers' study includes several other findings of interest. By the age of four the children in their study were averaging four hours of television a day. In general, the children watched more television as they got older. However, the average viewing time for girls decreased between four and five years of age, primarily because they watched less on Saturday morning. Finally, the Singers found a strong correlation between the amount of television watched and overt aggression in the classroom. Although this correlation does not prove that television watching causes children to be aggressive, it suggests that large doses of television watching do not help children discharge their aggressive feelings.

Chapter Six

The Adult as a Model
How parents and teachers
can join in imaginative play

In previous chapters we have included many examples of adults and children pretending together, and we have described the many ways in which adult participation increases the benefits of imaginative play. As active participants, adults provide children with opportunities to practice social skills, such as carrying on a conversation, coming to a compromise, and coping with teasing. Adults are a constant source of new ideas for improvising props, extending the plot, and organizing imaginary events into a logical sequence. Adults aid children in developing imaginary solutions to fears and support children in their search for creative symbols.

In this chapter we look further at the role of adults as models in imaginative play. In the first section we focus on the process by which adults discover that pretending with young children is fun. Most of the time parents join in pretending that is open-ended and spontaneous, but they can also initiate imaginative activities that are more structured. In the second section of this chapter we suggest several possibilities. These more structured activities are directed to teachers of young children. They could, however, be introduced at home as well, just as many of the practical suggestions we have made for pretending at home could be adapted to a school setting.

In the third section of this chapter we discuss how adults communicate their feelings and values by entering into imaginative play. Just as it is important for adults to observe children when playing with them, it is also beneficial for adults to become more aware of their own play styles and their own values. This increased knowledge about themselves leads to a pattern of interaction that is more rewarding both to themselves and to the children with whom they play.

HOW TO JOIN IN

It is common to find adults who feel awkward or foolish when they are asked to pretend with young children. If they can be persuaded to try, these same adults often find themselves having a good time. Feelings from their own childhood return as they relax and let their play instincts come to the surface.

The first rule of thumb for the reluctant adult pretender is to begin with an enjoyable activity. Some aspects of pretend play are not as appealing as others. Although adults want children to have fun, some adults find it difficult to participate in play that is wild and boisterous.

Consider imaginative play with toy cars as a case in point. Young children love to play with these cars, screeching around imaginary corners with their sirens on at full blast. It is rare to find an adult who wants to participate in this loud and reckless driving. An adult may join in by building a tunnel or bridge for the cars, but this is a limited and passive form of participation. Before adults can really be involved in car play, it must be restructured so that it is fun for them as well as for the children.

At Terry's home we collected some interesting examples. In one situation Terry's parents become the terrain over which Terry drives his toy car. This happens in the morning when Terry brings a car into his parents' bedroom and climbs on their bed. His mother turns into a road and his father becomes the mountains as Terry drives over the road to go exploring in the mountains.

A more elaborate routine involves racing toy cars. Terry and his father use an inclined desk blotter as the race track. Terry's father sets the scene, "Gentlemen, start your engines." A ruler holds the cars in place at the top of the blotter. Terry is instructed to give them the flag by dropping a handkerchief and Terry's father lifts the ruler:

Father: Who won the race?

Terry: Wonder Woman won that race.

Father: Which ones are going to race this time?

Terry: Let's try the black Volkswagen. I think Donald Duck is in it.

Father: Who is going to race against Donald?

Terry: Mickey Mouse.

Terry and his father at the races—the Tree Garden 500.

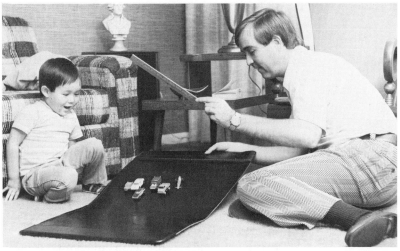

    Father: What shall we call this race?

    Terry: The Tree Garden 500.

    Not everyone is going to be like Terry's parents and find a way to enjoy playing with toy cars. Each person's sense of fun is his own. But these examples from Terry's family do illustrate how adults can extend a child's play in a way that makes the activity fun for adults. In one instance Terry's parents merely helped Terry expand an activity that he initiated—jumping on their bed in the morning with a toy car in his hand. Certainly many interesting side trips and rest stops come to mind when driving over a human body. In the other instance Terry's father introduced a structure for racing the cars. The structure seemed to appeal to him because he got to play the role of an announcer and because it involved conversation with Terry that he found interesting. Together they made up a name for the race, chose the cars, named the imaginary drivers, and discussed the winner.

    Our visit to Terry's house occurred at a single point in time. Perhaps Terry and his father will continue to enjoy racing toy cars together for quite a while. Perhaps Terry will take over the activity by himself, and his father's interest will turn to some new way of pretending. In order to maintain a sense of pleasure adults need to be honest with themselves. Sometimes an activity is fun for five or ten minutes but would be tedious for thirty. Other times an activity is very enjoyable for an adult the first few times but is boring after that. Adults who pretend with children inevitably find themselves invited to join activities that do not appeal to them. On occasion they may choose to indulge the children by playing anyway, but there is nothing wrong with informing a child that you do not feel like participating at that moment. In the long run children appreciate grown-up participation much more when adults are having fun too.

    Although no formulas exist that tell adults how to enjoy pretending with children, we can report some patterns that appeared in our visits. Among younger preschool children, two- and three-year-olds, adults were intrigued when they saw growth in the imitative skills of a child. All of us are captivated by a toddler who puts on an adult's hat or tries to walk in an adult's shoes. We smile when the child combs his hair with the back of a comb and brushes his teeth by sucking the toothpaste off the toothbrush. This ability to imitate blossoms rapidly, and it is all the more interesting when we are the people that are being copied.

    Jennifer's father was an avid photographer, and he was naturally quite pleased when Jennifer wanted to imitate him. Although the family's expensive camera was off limits, Jennifer was allowed to take pictures with the flash attachment. A few weeks later she got a toy camera, which was used to take pictures of everyone who came to the house. We asked Jennifer's father to take some pictures of Jennifer pretending. He was especially proud of a picture in which Jennifer stood poised over a ball with a golf club in her hand. Again she was imitating her father.

In the process of generalizing an imitative behavior, it becomes increasingly clear to children that their accomplishments are only pretend, that there is a qualitative difference between what they are doing and the real thing. The realization that there is such a thing as pretending is a very exciting discovery, and adults get a lot of pleasure teaching the idea to younger children.

For most adults the typical way to teach the idea of pretending is to imitate familiar actions themselves, especially the actions associated with eating. We see adults trying to drink from an empty cup or trying to feed a bit of food to a doll. When a young child seems to wonder why the cup is empty or why the food is not really eaten by the doll, the adults accompany their actions with an explanation that it is "just pretend."

In general, adults are not that excited about pretending to eat since they have a great deal of control over their real experiences with food. They decide when to eat, what to eat, and how much to eat. But during the period when a child becomes aware that it is possible to eat an imaginary meal of any description, adults join in with enthusiasm. The child's pleasure in discovering imaginative play is contagious.

In the same way, adults like to play with dolls when children are in the early stages of pretending. It is fun to help a two-year-old pretend to wash a doll's hair or pretend to clean its bottom because this way of playing is a new experience for the child. The teaching instincts of adults are stimulated, and they enjoy helping a child learn the range of possibilities in doll play. By the time children are four or five, adults are less likely to participate. The doll play is no longer a vehicle for learning about the ideas of pretending, and most adults are not highly disposed to take care of dolls because they have plenty of experience taking care of real children.

A particularly enjoyable way to teach the idea of pretending is through the use of books. Many young preschool children are intrigued by picture books. Pictures allow them to practice naming objects, and the children seem to be fascinated by the fact that the three dimensional world can be reduced to flat representations. If an adult uses these pictures to demonstrate imaginative play, young children usually respond quickly.

Preschool youngsters are intrigued with books.

"Do you like green eggs and ham?" said Amelia's mother as she pretended to pick a green egg off the page and feed it to Amelia. "Uh, uh," Amelia muttered, shaking her head emphatically in a negative gesture. "Oh, come on, just try one little bite," pleaded her mother, but still Amelia looked at the nonexistent egg in her mother's hand with obvious distaste. Later in the day they were looking at a picture in which a lion looked out from a cage. "Don't put your finger in there," said Amelia's mother, indicating the lion's mouth. "The lion will eat it up." But just as Amelia had refused to try a green egg, she now ignored this bit of parental advice. As she placed her finger on the lion's mouth her mother roared loudly. Startled for a brief moment Amelia then giggled and began to stick her finger on the lion's mouth again and again, just to hear him roar.

When playing with four- and five-year-old children, adults still enjoy being the teacher in a pretend situation. They are delighted with the emergence of a new pretend theme that gives them an opportunity to help their children learn. When adults feel the educational potential of a theme is exhausted, they tend to show less interest. Certain themes, however, continue to be replayed after they have lost their novelty. These are themes that touch strong feelings within an adult. Perhaps they bring back vivid memories of childhood. The list of favorite themes differs for every adult, but a few imaginative themes seem to have universal appeal.

144

SEEING THE DOCTOR

One of these themes is pretending to be sick and being treated by a doctor. When adults take the role of patient they invariably ask the pretend doctor in a worried voice, "What's wrong with me, doctor?" The answer confirms their fears—there is something wrong with them. Fortunately the diagnosis is quite benign and an instant cure is prescribed. Erik, for example, examined his father and declared that he had grass in his ear. This condition, Erik explained, came from eating a mud pie which had traveled up a little tube from his father's mouth to his ear. Erik administered three shots and a gumdrop pill—and his father was cured on the spot. Such medical magic appeals to the adult imagination as much as to the child's.

TAKING A TRIP

A second theme that adults especially enjoy is pretending to get away from the daily routine. It may be a camping trip, an evening at a restaurant, or a vacation to some faraway place. These special events represent escape from the normal schedule, and adults can give their own fantasies free rein. When the wishes of both adult and child find a common plane, they share such imaginary experiences with mutual pleasure.

GOING ON A SHOPPING SPREE

Most adults and children also have in common the fantasy of being able to buy anything at all. Danni and her mother played out a scene in an imaginary dress shop. Danni's mother played the part of the salesperson, assuring her five-year-old customer that all of the clothes in the store were very expensive. "That's all right. I have lots of charge cards," Danni replied, showing the salesperson some playing cards in her purse. A succession of scarves, shawls, and sweaters were tried on, and Danni decided to wear all of them at the same time. "Very smart," purred the salesperson. "How about this gorgeous hat?" she continued, putting an oversize felt hat on Danni that hid most of her head. Danni hesitated but the salesperson convinced her it was just right for the fancy ball she was attending that evening.

Although adults like to be extravagant customers too, they often end up being the salesperson because it is the harder part to play. Still they have plenty of opportunity to vent their feelings. Like Danni's mother, they can haggle with their young customers, drive hard bargains, or come up with a persuasive sale.

BEING A BAD GUY

A final role adults seem to enjoy playing is the part of a bad guy or monster. Every night when Ken and Jill's father came home, they hid because "the monster" was coming. Their father went looking for them with the intention of scaring them, but often they jumped out at him first. As we mentioned in earlier chapters, preschool children do not like to be robbers, but adults do seem to enjoy pretending to break the law. We can imagine the following scene would be fun for both adults and children. After stealing some toys and hiding them, the adult returns to his secret hideout (a favorite chair), where he is captured by the children. They put him in jail and search for the stolen toys, only to find that the robber has escaped from jail and is busy stealing something else.

STRUCTURED ACTIVITIES FOR THE CLASSROOM

In a school setting, the teacher may replace the parent as an active participant in imaginative play. Although many teachers enjoy pretending, their opportunities for participation may be limited by their need to supervise a number of children. In addition teachers may find find that children become overly excited when they join the play. The pretending of a peer group is so volatile that it tends to become chaotic if an adult adds extra stimulation by entering it. Teachers may feel that the level of noise and confusion is too high, and that the children will have difficulty accepting adult authority. The following guidelines will minimize this problem:

1. Make your participation a daily event so that the children are not overwhelmed by a sudden role change.
2. Orchestrate the classroom so that no more than four or five children are taking part in an imaginative play theme.
3. Assign the role you have been modeling to one of the children so that the play can continue after you leave the scene.

Given the limitations that teachers face, it remains true that young children eagerly seek the participation of teachers in their play. The children clearly feel positive about adult playmates in the classroom. For their part teachers may need to adopt a teaching role in order to feel comfortable with the peer group. A teacher can model a new role for the children, then step back and watch the children take over. Many of the prop suggestions made in the previous chapter require adult modeling in order to be successful. When a pretend store is first set up in the math center, for example, a teacher will probably need to model the role of storekeeper. When a new vehicle is created on the playground, the teacher may need to play the driver's part for the first few days.

Even when children have some idea how to get started, the teacher can show them how to elaborate and extend their play. We watched a teacher spend several weeks encouraging children to expand the theme of firefighter. This theme had appeared spontaneously in the classroom, but the children did not coordinate their ideas and there was little elaboration of the plot. The firefighter play was brief and episodic.

The teacher structured imaginative play around this theme in the following way. A small group of children was invited to play firefighter and each of them was asked to draw a picture of fire. After these colorful scribbles were completed, the teacher selected one child to help "start" a fire while the others waited at the fire station. The child with the teacher started the fire by taping his fire drawing on the wall somewhere in the room. Then he turned in the alarm by ringing a bell. This was the signal for the firefighters to come and put out the fire. When the children judged that the fire was extinguished, the teacher taped a large piece of black paper over the fire picture. In this way it was clear to everyone that the fire burned out and left nothing but black ashes.

Over a period of time, the teacher introduced other ideas—a long hose that required the cooperation of three or four children in putting out the fire, several dolls who had to be rescued from the fire, a ladder for climbing to "upper" stories of burning buildings. By suggesting, and even modeling, these new ideas the teacher succeeded in enriching the children's spontaneous play. When pretending by themselves, the children did not necessarily adopt the teacher's structured style of play, but they did begin to incorporate doll victims, alarm bells, ladders and fire hoses into the plot.

IMAGINATIVE PLAY WITH RECORDS

Music provides an opportunity of encouraging imaginative play with a relatively large group. The teacher may select from a variety of options in accordance with his or her own preference, and the needs, capabilities, and preferences of the children.

One option is to use records that are designed to promote imagination. These may be story records or sing-along records. A second option involves the use of rhythm instruments to accompany a narrative poem. An old favorite in this genre is "I'm going on a bear hunt," where the teacher says the words and the children beat out the rhythm and perform the appropriate actions.

A third option is the use of mood music or rhythm where the sounds set the mood for pretending. In this situation the teacher may make suggestions like:

"Let's pretend we are marching like elephants.
It's very cold, and the wind is blowing.
You are a top spinning round and round.
You are a tree blowing in the wind; you are a flower growing
    upward toward the sky.
You are carrying a heavy package and you are moving very
    slowly."

Moving to music can also be a child-directed activity where the children make suggestions about what they would like to pretend. Sometimes children enjoy listening to the mood of the music and dancing or swaying in a way that reflects this mood. A favorite activity in some classrooms is waving silk scarves in time with the music. Larger swatches of material permit tandem or small group movement activities.

ART AND IMAGINATIVE PLAY ACTIVITIES

An art center is inevitably a place where children express their imagination. As we have discussed in earlier chapters, much of a preschool child's drawing and painting does not represent an exploration of an imaginary theme. Rather it is an exploration of color and form

Moving to music.

possibilities. The development of an imaginary theme may come after the picture is completed.

Whether or not a child has preplanned a drawing, there are many instances in which children want to talk to a teacher about their finished picture. Teachers have been advised to avoid labeling a child's artwork and it is wise to be cautious. Children sometimes wish to leave a drawing as a design, but more often they want to see something in it. Once they give a teacher some clue as to what the picture represents, they greatly enjoy an imaginative interpretation on the teacher's part. They like to speculate along with the teacher about the name of a pictured character, the whereabouts of the character's mother, the way the character is feeling, etc.

Older preschool children are able to organize these speculations into a coherent story. When a picture leads to a memorable story, teachers can write the story down. If a story does not materialize, children may want the teacher to write a title that summarizes the conversation, such as "Eastern Airplane at Southern Airport," or "Holiday Inn on Fire."

Imaginative play based on art does not need to be confined to a child's artwork. Teachers too like to draw. A teacher can start a drawing by creating a major character and then let interested children add details. For example, before Easter the teacher might draw an Easter Bunny on a large piece of paper, put it up in the art center, and then see if eggs, baskets, candy, and flowers are added by interested children. Or, a teacher can draw a more complete picture with empty balloons above the characters. Interested children can make up dialogue to be written in the balloons.

The art center also can serve as a place to create props for imaginative play in other parts of the room. Paper bag masks or simple costumes can be made for role play. Paper plates can be decorated with food pictures for use in a pretend restaurant. Rubber stamps and markers can be used to make money for pretending. Wood chips can be glued together and painted for use as miniature buildings or furniture.

PUPPET PLAY

Puppetry is another kind of activity that can be used to promote imaginative play. Puppets can be purchased that represent television characters, community helpers, or storybook characters; or puppets can be made by teachers and children out of simple material like socks, gloves, or paper bags.

A puppet can start a conversation with a group of children:

Bert: (Animated by teacher) So I decided to go out to play football and what do you think I brought along?

Children: A football—

Bert: Yes, I should have taken a football but I forgot it. But guess what I did bring along? It's something to eat.

Or the children can be given puppets and the teacher can initiate a dialogue with a child's puppet.

Teacher: Hello, my name is Oscar Noisemaker. What is your name?

1st Child: (Talking for puppet) My name is Oscar too.

Teacher: No, no. Oscar is my name. That puppet took away my name.

1st Child: I did not take your name. Oscar is my name.

Teacher: (Turning to another child) Did you take my Noisemaker?

2nd Child: No.

Teacher: Where is my Noisemaker? I need some noise. (Turning to a child with a kitten puppet) Can you make me a cat noise?

3rd Child: Meow.

"My name is Oscar Noisemaker."

Teacher: That meow was too soft. Puppets, when I bow my head let me hear a big meow. Oh, my, I just heard a duck quack. Is there a duck in this room?

A third way to use puppets is for the teacher to talk to the puppet as if it were a child. This is particularly useful when the teacher is dealing with potential fears. The following dialogue was used by a teacher the day before the dentist's visit:

Teacher: (to clown puppet) Clown, why are you hiding under the pillows?

Clown: Because the dentist is coming.

Teacher: The dentist is not coming today. He is coming tomorrow.

Clown: I don't want the dentist to come and I'm hiding here until tomorrow comes. The dentist won't find me under the pillow.

Teacher: You are being silly. The dentist is not going to hurt you.

Clown: He's going to pull out all my teeth.

Teacher: You're a silly clown. The dentist isn't going to pull your teeth. All he is going to do is brush your teeth with fluoride and that doesn't hurt one little bit.

Teachers can use puppets to loosen up the reading of a story. The puppet can ask children questions or make side comments as the teacher reads the story. In this way, the reading of a story becomes an occasion for adult-child conversation. Puppets also can be used to act out stories the children hear, or they can inspire new stories by the children. The Muppet characters from "Sesame Street" are especially appropriate for this purpose.

From watching television children are familiar with scenes involving these characters, and they understand the personality of each one. Ernie is the joker who always is tricking his serious friend Bert. Cookie Monster is lovable but insatiably hungry. Oscar is grouchy and loves dirt. Grover tries to do everything and as a result gets into a lot of trouble.

A set of these puppets can be used to reenact skits from television, as well as to generate scenes that speak to the feelings of preschool children. We can imagine Bert having to share Ernie with another friend, or Oscar being grouchy because of sibling jealousy. Grover's mother could appear when Grover makes a mess and breaks things, or Big Bird could have a Little Bird who is fearful about being separated from its mother. The teacher could use the puppets to set the problem, and then the puppets could appeal to the children for help in solving their dilemmas.

BOOKS AND IMAGINATIVE PLAY

Looking at books is in itself an imaginative experience. Sometimes children enter into the imaginary story created by the author. More often they use the pictures to generate their own fantasies. Encyclopedias are used this way by preschool children. A picture of a whale leads to a conversation between children about sharks, whales, and all kinds of other sea creatures. Information is shared along with fears, wishes, and lies.

Stories from books can be used as the basis for simple plays. Putting on a dramatic performance is a technique frequently used around holiday time. The teacher reads a story or recites a nursery rhyme, and the children select their own roles. The performance works best if the script is flexible. Even if there are three Goldilocks or several Snow Whites, it is the process that is more important than the product.

Once children understand the idea of a play, they enjoy dictating short scripts. We visited a classroom in which the rule was that the author of a play got to assign all the roles. Later, during large group time, the teacher read the play one sentence at a time. As each sentence was read the cast carried out the appropriate actions to the delight of the rest of the class. John had written the following play and then assigned the parts to himself and to his friends:

> The robber went North and saw Superman and the bear.
> He went South. The bear eats up the robber.
> Robber—Jason
> Superman—John
> Bear—Mark

From time to time the entire reading center can be turned into a pretend library. This seems a particularly good way to introduce the reading center at the beginning of the year. After a visit to the real library, the children can make pretend library cards and take turns checking books in and out. A teacher can model how librarians help children find books that interest them, and the pretend setting can be used to reinforce the rules for handling books in the classroom. Children can be encouraged to "read" stories to each other or to dolls as they sit in the library. They can make their own volumes for the library by pasting pictures in small, homemade books.

TRANS-MITTING VALUES

Whenever adults influence imaginative play, whether by providing props, participating directly, or setting limits, they communicate their values to the children. Through their interest adults tell children that it is good to develop friendships, that it is valuable to grow intellectually, and that it is important to feel good about yourself. The way an adult enters into imaginative play will communicate the relative value that is placed on these various benefits. Let us look at three mothers whose styles of play differed noticeably.

THE SOCIAL PRETENDER

The pretending of Wendy and her mother usually revolves around ordinary, everyday events: cooking, selling Avon products, going bowling. On our visit to their home we watched them play restaurant and beauty shop. It was notable that nothing of much consequence happened in these scenes. At the restaurant Wendy was the waitress and served her mother an undistinguished meal of meat and potatoes. At the beauty shop she combed her mother's hair, then pretended to cut and blow dry it. Throughout their play the conversation was low-keyed chitchat. Wendy's mother seemed to focus on having a relaxed social encounter with her daughter. She did not try to introduce any novel ideas or get Wendy in an excited state. The result was a pleasant atmosphere with no hint of tension or competition between parent and child.

THE INTELLECTUAL PRETENDER

Laura and her mother's favorite theme is shopping at the mall. Different kinds of merchandise are available in various rooms of the house. There is a toy department, a furniture department, a housewares department, a stationery department, etc. The kitchen becomes a restaurant at the mall, the bathroom is a public restroom in a store, and a large closet serves as the elevator. We observed one of these mother-daughter mall excursions and recorded the dialogue. As we went back over our notes we were struck by the number of times Laura's mother changed the direction of the play by introducing new ideas. Here are some typical excerpts:

> "Would you like to play mall? . . .
> Here's some water for us to drink. Do we need menus? . . . It looks like this fork is dirty . . .
> What is the name of this restaurant? . . . I spilled some coffee on my menu. I need more . . . Oh, look who is in the restaurant. Daddy is here. Margo (the dog) is here. . . .

153

Shall we go to the toy department? . . .
Do you have money? . . .
Do you want to pack up your purchases? . . .
Let us go look at the dresses. Let's go to the elevator . . .
Here we are on the second floor. I'd like to try the lipstick. Here's
a perfect shade for you. . . ."

Laura's mother also incorporates many props into the play. When eating a pretend lunch Laura and her mother use real dishes. They shop for a real watch, real dresses, a real bed, etc. By introducing a variety of questions and props Laura's mother encourages a kind of imaginative play that is intellectually complex. She keeps the play moving forward by introducing new ideas, and the resulting atmosphere is intense and exciting.

THE THERAPEUTIC PRETENDER

Kori's mother aims for a different type of complexity. Her style of participation is to use imaginative play to talk about Kori's feelings. She tells stories to Kori in which the main character is Kori in disguise. Kori realizes that the main character in these "Kori stories" is herself, and she has begun to request such a story by taking on a new identity:

> *Kori:* Hi, Mommy. What's your name?
>
> *Mother:* My name is Betty. What's your name?
>
> *Kori:* (Playing with a rubber duck) My name is Nosey. Tell me a story.
>
> *Mother:* Is there any particular story you would like?
>
> *Kori:* I want the one about me.
>
> *Mother:* Okay. What do you do in the story?
>
> *Kori:* I play with blocksies.

Given this clue Kori's mother tells a story about Nosey the duck having his block tower knocked down at playgroup. She describes how Nosey feels and how he resolves to protect his blocks next time. The story mirrors an upsetting incident Kori recently has experienced.

Kori and her mother also pretend by playing out a ritualized dialogue. Kori's mother plays the part of Raggie (a doll) while Kori is Raggie's mother. In effect Kori and her mother engage in a kind of role reversal that is typical of parents and three-year-olds, except that in this case the pretending reflects the special style of Kori's mother. The play focuses on Kori's feelings and is cast in the form of a dramatic story.

> *Kori:* Ask Raggie why she's crying.
>
> *Mother:* Raggie, why are you crying?
>
> *Kori:* You say.
>
> *Raggie:* (Kori's mother speaking) I'm hungry.
>
> *Kori:* You already had breakfast, but you didn't take your vitamin seed and your pills.
>
> *Raggie:* Where is it?
>
> *Kori:* It's in the freezer.
>
> *Raggie:* Well, I can't open it.
>
> *Kori:* Get your little stool from the bathroom and you will be able to reach it. Now open the bottle.
>
> *Raggie:* I can't.
>
> *Kori:* Yes you can. It's not hard, Raggie. Just unwind it. Spill it in your hand.

We can infer from this example that Kori has been complaining that she can't do this or that. By transferring the same feelings to Raggie, Kori's mother helps Kori understand her own behavior and cope with her own negative feelings.

All three of these mothers enjoy pretending with their children, but each one focused on a different function of imaginative play. Wendy's mother was most attuned to the social function of imaginative play. Laura's mother emphasized the intellectual side of pretending. Kori's mother stressed the emotional value of pretending. The function that each one valued the most came through in the style of play.

Despite the differences in style, parents and teachers who join in imaginative play seem to share two overriding values. First, they want children to develop the feeling that they are important, powerful individuals. They want children to have confidence in their own ideas, to take part in decision making, and to become adept at solving their own problems. Second, they want children to develop a feeling of compassion, to be considerate and cooperative. In practice these two values are not always easy to reconcile.

A common technique for giving children the feeling that they are powerful individuals is for adults to take a subordinate role in imaginative play. Chad and his mother provide a striking example. They played a game in which Chad's mother becomes a pony named Jelly Bean Charlie and Chad becomes its master. Chad feeds Jelly Bean Charlie water and sugar cubes, but most of the time he leads the faithful horse around the house on all fours. One day we even saw him walking his mother up and down the sidewalk. Chad certainly realizes that his role as master is limited to imaginative play. But even though he cannot be the boss in many real situations, he knows that his mother supports his desire to be a more powerful person.

When adult authority has to be exercised, parents who value pretending often turn to imaginative play so their children will not feel put down. For example, Erik and his parents reduce conflict with a kind of pretending based on verbal nonsense.

When Erik resists going to bed, his parents ask him a series of questions like, "Is your elbow sleepy? Is your nose sleepy? Are your toes sleepy?" The questions elicit a mounting crescendo of no's from Erik. Finally they ask, "Well, what is sleepy?", and Erik fairly yells "Nothing." Following this outburst of imaginary anger Erik is more willing to face the bed.

On another occasion Erik did not want to go shopping with his parents. "Okay," said his father, "You stay home and Mama and I will go out and eat chocolate ice cream." "I want to go too," Erik chimed in quickly. "You do?" his father asked in disbelief. "You've changed your mind? Okay, you go out and I will stay home and eat chocolate pudding." "I want chocolate pudding," wailed Erik. "You do? You've changed your mind again?" his father answered. "Well, then, you stay home and Mama and I will go to the beach." Back and forth went the exchange with Erik realizing more and more that his father was just pretending. And in the process of discovering this fact, Erik forgot about his original complaint.

Although adults who join in imaginative play want children to gain a sense of power, they are disturbed when children pretend to be aggressive or violent. In particular, the use of guns in imaginative play is frequently a source of conflict between children and adults. In order to continue using the guns, children may deny that they are hurting anyone:

> *Mother:* What are you making?
>   *Kori:* A gun.
> *Mother:* What is your gun for?
>   *Kori:* It's for shooting bad people.
> *Mother:* I don't think there are people bad enough to be shot. I

don't like guns because they can hurt people and scare people.

Kori: This gun is for shooting bad wolves.

Mother: That's okay, but real wolves aren't bad. Just wolves in stories are bad.

Kori: Mommy, if we read the story of Little Red Riding Hood I'm going to shoot the wolf.

Mother: That's a good idea. What will happen to the wolf if you shoot him?

Kori: He's not going to get dead. I am just going to shoot him out of the meadow and into the forest.

Using a gun may even become a very civilized procedure. When we visited Ken's house, we found him using broomsticks and rulers for guns, since he was not allowed to play with toy guns. He threatened, in a very polite and pleasant manner, to shoot us with a yardstick. He sounded almost apologetic. Since we did not want to be shot, he pointed his homemade gun at a stuffed dog and said quietly, "Bang—I shot you." Even this act of violence had to be covered up. Asked if the dog was dead, Ken replied, "Oh, no, he's just sleeping."

In joining imaginative play adults try to communicate a balance between two primary values—being strong and being compassionate. The following story, which was a favorite in Kori's family, reflects this sense of balance. In the world of imagination everyone has a place of dignity, and conflicts are solved peacefully:

Once upon a time the Sun and Moon started to fight. And they kept fighting and fighting.

Their friend the Cloud came over to find out what all the fighting was about. "Why are you fighting?" asked the Cloud.

"I'm big and bright," said the Sun. "I should be the only thing that shines in the sky."

"No, no," said the Moon. "I'm small and pretty. I should be the only thing that shines in the sky."

"Oh, my," said the Cloud. "If you can't get along you'll have to be separated. Sun, you can shine in the sky during the day, and everyone will say how big and bright you are. And Moon, you can shine in the sky at night and everyone will say how small and pretty you are."

"That's a terrible idea," said the Moon. "I will never see my friend the Sun." "That's a terrible idea," said the Sun. "I will never see my friend the Moon."

"I'll tell you what," said the Cloud. "When you're lonesome you can visit each other and I will hide you."

"That's a wonderful idea," said the Sun and Moon.

So the Sun took his turn in the daytime and the Moon took her turn in the nighttime, and every once in a while the Moon hid behind the Cloud in the daytime and visited her friend the Sun, and the Sun hid behind the Cloud in the nighttime and visited with his friend the Moon. And the Sun and the Moon were very good friends and they didn't fight anymore.

FROM THE LITERATURE

Quotations from the book *From Two to Five* by Kornei Chukovsky, on the subject of "topsy-turvies":*

The child plays not only with marbles, with blocks, with dolls, but also with ideas. No sooner does he master some idea than he is only too eager to make it his toy.... When my two-year-old daughter forced the imaginary dog to meow, she was playing this kind of game. To participate in this game, I immediately composed a whole series of similar topsy turvies:

The piglet meowed—
Meow! Meow!

The kittens oinked—
Oink! Oink!

I felt like a carpenter who had shaped a toy for his child.... (pp. 98–99)

The facetious description of the tiny and the lightweight in terms of the huge and the heavy is one of the most widely used types of topsy-turvies in children's folklore. In an English folksong Simple Simon casts a fishing rod into a small pail and pulls out a whale. In another, from the same group, a "squad" of tailors, numbering twenty-four, sail on a snail

*Kornei Chukovsky, *From Two to Five*, translated by Miriam Morton (Berkeley: University of California Press, 1963).

and no sooner does the small snail reveal its horns than they scatter in fright.... (pp. 101–102)

This nonsense would be dangerous for children only if it obscured from them the authentic and the real interrelations of ideas and things. But not only do topsy-turvies not obscure them, they make them clearer, color them, and underscore them. They strengthen (not weaken) the child's awareness of reality. This gives the nonsense of topsy-turvies its educational value. (p. 104)

This inquisitive and ambitious explorer of the world (the young child) must feel great joy when it becomes clear to him that vast regions of knowledge have already been permanently conquered by him, and that errors are made by others but not by him. Others do not seem to know that there is ice only in winter, that it is impossible to burn one's tongue with cold porridge, that the cat does not fear mice. (p. 102)

PART THREE

AFTERTHOUGHTS

"No, no!" said the Queen. "Sentence first—verdict afterwards."
"Stuff and nonsense!" said Alice loudly. "The idea of having the
sentence first!"

"Hold your tongue!" said the Queen, turning purple.

"I won't!" said Alice.

"Off with her head!" the Queen shouted at the top of her voice.
Nobody moved.

"Who cares for you?" said Alice (she had grown to her full size by
this time). "You're nothing but a pack of cards!"

Like Alice in Wonderland we are ready to make our way out of
the rabbit hole. We cannot agree with Alice, however, that the fantasies
of children are no more than "a pack of cards." We have seen over and
over again that the pretend world young children create is a substantial
part of their lives. In this chapter we want to summarize our findings by
relating them to the theoretical issues and empirical findings discussed
in the research literature.

The value of imaginative play is strongly supported in the research literature. A positive correlation has been reported between
pretending and a host of desirable qualities, such as intelligence,
creativity, impulse control, positive affect, and communication skills.
The literature goes beyond mere association. A series of intervention
studies have replicated the finding that training or encouraging children to pretend actually causes a significant increase in positive behaviors and traits.

The first three chapters of *Just Pretending* discussed how pretending helps children achieve social skills, make sense of the world,
and satisfy their emotional needs. All of these functions have been
described in some form as outcomes of imaginative play training. Intervention studies have shown that pretending makes children more
friendly and cooperative, helps children develop emotional control,
and improves performance on intelligence and creativity tests.

The intervention studies have other implications as well. They
demonstrate the importance of the role of the adult in imaginative play.
A modest investment of time by a few adults can pay off in recognizable changes for a whole classroom of children. The intervention
studies suggest that giving children the space, equipment, and time to
pretend is not sufficient. Adult modeling seems to be necessary to raise
pretending above an elementary and sporadic level. At the same time
the intervention studies indicate that young children have a strong
latent ability to pretend. A little modeling goes a long way. It is an

interesting paradox. Preschool children apparently are intellectually and emotionally ready to burst into imaginative play, but adult encouragement and participation are needed to ignite the process.

Many of the adults we visited were very involved in the imaginative play of two- and three-year-old children. Even among older preschool children, adults were the primary companions when complex themes were played out. In fact, it could be concluded that the high level of imaginative play among the children in our study is attributable in large part to the involvement of significant adults. The intervention studies suggest that adults should be encouraged to pretend with young children, and the descriptions of parent-child play we have shared give us confidence that with a little encouragement all parents and teachers would enjoy pretending with children.

Included in the current literature is a debate about the way imaginative play fits into the overall development of a child. Piaget argues that imaginative play is characterized by preoperational thought. According to his theory the framework preschool children use to interpret experience is unstable because the children have not learned to distinguish between feelings and concepts. They cannot adequately separate themselves as thinkers from their thoughts about the world. The reason imaginative play appeals so much to preschool children is that their feelings and ideas can coexist in harmonious confusion. Fears or unfulfilled wishes can be projected into a familiar reality, and at the same time new ideas about reality can be explored within a context of emotional security.

Piaget's theoretical position on imaginative play, which was developed thirty years ago, is being compared to another theory of the same vintage by Vygotsky. Vygotsky's essential point is that imaginative play is a social activity in the sense that it is a form of communication. As children pretend, the collective wishes of the group are communicated to them by adults and other children. At the same time they learn to communicate through the use of language, gestures, and symbolic objects. Vygotsky especially emphasizes the importance of symbolic objects in helping children to recognize that the relationship between a symbol and a referent can be arbitrary. According to Vygotsky's view, this insight is critical, for as symbols are separated from reality the way is open for abstract thinking.

Piaget looks at pretending from the viewpoint of the individual. Because he focuses on the individual, his theory highlights the way pretending meets the emotional needs of young children. Certainly there is abundant evidence in our study that pretending serves this purpose. Invisible playmates are interjected into lonely or stressful situations, fears are played out in totally safe environments, new experiences are replayed with the confident knowledge that they can be discontinued at any time.

On the other hand, there is plenty of evidence that Vygotsky's view is valid also. The children we visited were learning the ways of society as they pretended. Every imaginative play setting, whether taking care of a baby, eating a pretend meal, or going on a shopping trip, involved the communication of cultural norms. The communication skills of the children were growing too. Most of the pretend episodes we described were social, and they were understood by everyone involved. Symbolic objects and gestures helped communicate what was happening, but language was the primary means for establishing a consensus. Even when children played by themselves other imaginary characters usually took part, and the children used language to set the stage and guide the play.

Pretending can be seen as an individual phenomenon or a collective phenomenon. Both perspectives are useful. In a larger sense the difference between Piaget and Vygotsky represents two motifs from a single theme. Piaget and Vygotsky both stress that imaginative play involves the development of symbolic thinking and that this step ultimately leads to the ability to think abstractly and logically.

Most adults would agree with Piaget and Vygotsky that imaginative play provides a nurturing climate for the growth of young children. Still, some parents and teachers have a nagging fear. If children are too involved in pretending will they still be interested in the academic lessons of school? James Snyder, a six-year-old boy, gives us his answer:

> The wind was bringing me to school
> And that is the fast way to get to school.
> So why don't you let the wind bring you
> to school just like me? And you will be
> in school on time, just like I was.*

BOOKS TO READ TO CHILDREN

ANGLUND, JOAN WALSH. *In a Pumpkin Shell.* New York: Harcourt Brace Jovanvich, Inc., 1960.

BEMELMANS, LUDWIG. *Madeline and the Gypsies.* New York: Viking, 1957.

BERENSTAIN, STAN AND JAN. *The Berenstain Bears Go to School.* New York: Random House, 1978.

BOND, MICHAEL. *A Bear Called Paddington.* New York: Dell Pub. Co., Inc., 1976.

BONI, MARGARET AND LLOYD, NORMAN. *Fireside Book of Folk Songs.* New York: Simon & Schuster, 1966.

BRADFIELD, JOAN AND ROGER. *Who Are You?* Racine, Wis.: Whitman Publishing Co., Inc. 1966.

BROWN, MARCIA. *The Three Billy Goats Gruff.* New York: Harcourt Brace Jovanovich, 1957.

BROWN, MARGARET WISE. *The City Noisy Book.* New York: Harper & Row, Pub., 1940.

———. *The Country Noisy Book.* New York: Harper & Row, Pub., 1940.

———. *The Dead Bird.* Reading, Mass.: Addison-Wesley, 1958.

———. *Goodnight Moon.* New York: Harper & Row, Pub., 1947.

———. *The Runaway Bunny.* New York: Harper & Row, Pub., 1942.

CARLE, ERIC. *The Very Hungry Caterpillar.* New York: Collins Publishers, 1970.

COLLIER, ETHEL. *The Birthday Tree.* Reading, Mass.: Addison-Wesley, 1975.

DEBRUNHOFF, JEAN. *Babar the King.* New York: Random House, 1937.

DENNIS, WESLEY. *Flip and the Morning.* New York: Viking, 1951.

EASTMAN, P. D. *Are You My Mother?* Boston, Mass.: Little, Brown, 1975.

FREEMAN, DON. *Beady Bear.* New York: Viking, 1954.

FUJIKAWA, GYO. *Betty Bear's Birthday.* Japan: Zokeisha Publishing, Ltd., 1977.

———. *Come Follow Me.* New York: Grosset & Dunlap, 1979.

GAULKE, GLORIA. *Where is My Shoe?* New York: Holt, Rinehart and Winston, Inc., 1965.

GOBLE, PAUL. *The Girl Who Loved Wild Horses.* Scarsdale, N.Y.: Bradbury Press, 1978.

HARGREAVER, ROGER. *Mr. Happy.* Los Angeles: Price/Stern/Sloan Publishers, Inc., 1971.

HAZEN, BARBARA SHOCK. *To Be Me.* Elgin, Ill.: The Child's World, Inc., 1975.

KEATS, EZRA JACK. *Goggles.* New York: Macmillan, 1971.

———. *The Snowy Day.* New York: Viking, 1962.

———. *Whistle for Willie.* New York: Viking, 1964.

KENT, JACK. *The Egg Book.* New York: Macmillan, 1975.

KRAUSS, RUTH. *Bears.* New York: Harper & Row, Pub., 1948.

———. *The Carrot Seed.* New York: Harper & Row, Pub., 1945.

———. *A Hole is to Dig.* New York: Harper & Row, Pub., 1952.

———. *I'll Be You and You Be Me.* New York: Harper & Row, Pub., 1954.

LAMORISSE, A. *The Red Balloon.* New York: Doubleday, 1956.

LEAR, EDWARD. *The Owl and The Pussy Cat.* London: Jonathan Cape.

LE SIEG, THEO. *In a People House.* New York: Random House, 1972.

LOBEL, ARNOLD. *Frog and Toad Are Friends.* New York: Harper & Row, Pub., 1970.

MACPHERSON, ELIZABETH. *A Tale of Tails.* Racine, Wis.: Golden Press.

MARZOLLO, JEAN. *Close Your Eyes.* New York: Dial Press, 1978.

MATHEWS, GEDA BRADLEY. *What Was That!* Racine, Wis.: Western Publishing Co., Inc., 1977.

MCCLOSKEY, ROBERT. *Make Way for Ducklings.* New York: Viking, 1969.

———. *One Morning in Maine.* New York: Viking, 1952.

MCCORD, DAVID. *The Star in the Pail.* Boston, Mass.: Little, Brown, 1925.

MCNAUGHT, HARRY. *Animal Babies.* New York: Random House, 1977.

MILNE, A. A. *Winnie the Pooh.* New York: Dutton, 1926.

MITGUTSCHM, ALI. *The Busy Book.* Racine, Wis.: Western Publishing Co., Inc., 1976.

PARISH, PEGGY. *Good Work, Amelia Bedelia.* New York: Avon Books, 1976.

PERKINS, AL. *The Digging-est Dog.* New York: Random House, 1967.

PERL, SUSAN. *Let's Play.* New York: Platt & Munk.

POTTER, BEATRIX. *Cecily Parsley's Nursery Rhymes.* London: F. Warne & Co., Ltd. 1922.

———. *The Tale of Peter Rabbit.* London: F. Warne & Co., Ltd. 1902.

POULET, VIRGINIA. *Blue Bug's Treasure.* Chicago: Children's Press, 1976.

SCARRY, RICHARD. *Richard Scarry's Best Word Book Ever.* Racine, Wis.: Western Publishing Co., Inc., 1963.

———. *The Funniest Storybook Ever.* New York: Random House, 1972.

———. *I Am a Bunny.* Racine, Wis.: Golden Press, 1963.

———. *Richard Scarry's Best Story Book Ever.* Racine, Wis.: Western Publishing Co., Inc., 1968.

———. *Cars & Trucks & Things That Go.* Racine, Wis.: Western Publishing Co., Inc., 1974.

SEEGER, RUTH, comp. *American Folk Songs for Children.* New York: Doubleday, 1948.

SENDAK, MAURICE. *Hector Protector and As I Went Over the Water.* New York: Harper & Row, Pub., 1967.

———. *Higglety Pigglety Pop: or There Must Be More to Life.* New York: Harper & Row, Pub., 1967.

———. *In The Night Kitchen.* New York: Harper & Row, Pub., 1970.

———. *Kenny's Window.* New York: Harper & Row, Pub., 1956.

———. *Where the Wild Things Are.* New York: Harper & Row, Pub., 1940.

SEUSS, DR. *Green Eggs & Ham.* New York: Random House, 1968.

———. *How the Grinch Stole Christmas.* New York: Random House, 1957.

———. *Horton Hatches the Egg.* New York: Random House, 1940.

———. *If I Ran the Circus.* New York: Random House, 1956.

SIMON, NORMA. *Why Am I Different?* Chicago: Albert Whitman & Co., 1976.

STEVENSON, ROBERT LOUIS. *A Child's Garden of Verses.* New York: Random House, 1978.

TUDOR, TASHA. *Wings For the Wind.* Philadelphia: Lippincott, 1964.

WEZEL, PETER. *The Good Birds.* New York: Harper & Row, Pub., 1966.

BIBLIOGRAPHY

ALMY, M. *The Early Childhood Educator at Work.* New York: McGraw-Hill, 1975.

ARNHEIM, RUDOLF. *Visual Thinking.* Berkeley: University of California Press, 1969.

BETTLEHEIM, BRUNO. *The Uses of Enchantment.* New York: Vintage Books, 1977.

BIBER, B. *Children's Drawings.* New York: Bank Street College of Education, 1932.

BJORKLUND, GAIL. *Planning for Play: A Developmental Approach.* Columbus, Ohio: Chas. E. Merrill, 1978.

BUTLER, ANNE, EDWARD GOTTS, AND NANCY QUESENBERRY. *Play as Development.* Columbus, Ohio: Chas. E. Merrill, 1978.

COBB, EDITH. *The Ecology of Imagination in Childhood.* New York: Columbia University Press, 1977.

FEITELSON, D., AND G. S. ROSS. "Neglected Factor: Play," *Human Development,* 16 (1973), 202–23.

FLAVELL, JOHN H. *The Development of Role-Taking and Communication Skills in Children.* New York: John Wiley, 1968.

GARVEY, CATHERINE. *The Developing Child.* Cambridge, Mass.: Harvard University Press, 1977.

GETZELS, J. W., AND P. W. JACKSON. *Creativity and Intelligence.* New York: John Wiley, 1962.

GOLDSTEIN, J. H., AND P. E. MCGHEE, eds. *The Psychology of Humor.* New York: Academic Press, 1972.

GOODNOW, JACQUELINE. "Children's Drawings," in *The Developing Child,* edited by Jerome Bruner, Michael Cole, Barbara Lloyd. Cambridge, Mass.: Harvard University Press, 1977.

GOULD, ROSALIND. *Child Studies Through Fantasy.* New York: Quadrangle, 1972.

GUILFORD, J. P. *Intelligence, Creativity and Their Educational Implication.* San Diego, Calif.: Robert Knapp, 1968.

HARTLEY, R. E., L. C. FRANK AND R. M. GOLDENSON. *Understanding Children's Play.* New York: Columbia University Press, 1952.

HERRON, R. E., AND B. SUTTON-SMITH. *Child's Play.* New York: John Wiley, 1971.

HOBAN, TANA. *Dig, Drill, Dump, Fill.* New York: Morrow, 1975.

HOROVITZ, HILDA LEWIS, AND MARK LUCA. *Understanding Children's Art for Better Teaching.* Columbus, Ohio: Chas. E. Merrill, 1967.

ISAACS, SUSAN. *The Children We Teach.* London: University of London Press, Ltd., 1950.

KEATS, EZRA JACK. *The Trip.* New York: Morrow Jr. Books, 1978.

KELLOGG, RHODA. *Analyzing Children's Art.* Palo Alto, Calif.: National Press, 1969.

KNAPP, MARY AND HERBERT KNAPP. *One Potato, Two Potato: The Folklore of American Children.* New York: W. W. Norton and Co., Inc., 1976.

KRAUSS, RUTH. *Somebody Spilled the Sky.* New York: Morrow, 1979.

LEWIS, RICHARD, ed. *Miracles: Poems by Children of the English-Speaking World.* New York: Simon & Schuster, 1966.

LIEBERMAN, J. NINA. *Playfulness, Its Relationship to Imagination and Creativity.* New York: Academic Press, 1977.

MATTHEWS, WENDY SCHEMPP. "Sex Role Perception, Portrayal and Preference in the Fantasy Play of Young Children." Paper presented at the Biennial Meeting of the Society for Research in Child Development, March 17–20, 1977, New Orleans, La.

PIAGET, JEAN. *Play, Dreams and Imitation in Childhood.* New York: W. W. Norton and Co., Inc., 1962.

——. *The Origins of Intelligence in Children.* New York: International Universities Press, Inc., 1953.

PULASKI, M. A., "Play as a Foundation of Toy Structure and Fantasy Predisposition," *Child Development* 41 (1970), 531–37.

ROSEN, C. E., "The Effects of Sociodramatic Play on Problem Solving Behavior among Culturally Disadvantaged Preschool Children," *Child Development* 45 (1974), 920–27.

SALTZ, ELI, DAVID DIXON, AND JAMES JOHNSON, "Training Disadvantaged Preschoolers on Various Fantasy Activities, Effects on Cognitive Functioning and Impulse Control." *Child Development* 48 (1977), 367–80.

SINGER, J. L. *The Child's World of Make-Believe.* New York: Academic Press, 1973.

SMILANSKY, S. *The Effects of Sociodramatic Play on Disadvantaged Preschool Children.* New York: John Wiley, 1968.

SMITH, NANCY R., AND MARGAREY B. FRANKLIN. *Symbolic Functioning in Childhood.* New York: John Wiley, 1979.

SPONSELLER, DORIS, ed. *Play as a Learning Medium.* Washington, D.C.: National Association for the Education of Young Children, 1974.

SUTTON-SMITH, BRIAN. *Play and Learning.* New York: Gardner Press, 1979.

VYGOTSKY, L. "Play and Its Role in the Mental Development of the Child." *Soviet Psychology,* 5 (1967), 6–18.

WEININGER, OTTO. *Play and Education.* Springfield, Ill.: Chas. C Thomas, 1979.

WHITE, JAMES. *Talking with a Child.* New York: Macmillan, 1976.

WOLF, DENNIE. "Early Symbolization." In *New Directions for Child Development,* edited by William Damon. San Francisco: Jossey-Bass, 1979.

Index

DATE DUE

MAR 8 '83			
NO 06 '92			